Sweet Corn Spectacular

Minnesota Historical
Society Press

Sweet Corn Spectacular

Marie Porter

the *N*orthern plate

the orthern plate

Sweet Corn Spectacular is the third book in the Northern Plate series, celebrating the bounty of the Upper Midwest by focusing on a single ingredient, exploring its historical uses as well as culinary applications across a range of dishes. *Rhubarb Renaissance* by Kim Ode and *Modern Maple* by Teresa Marrone are other books in the series.

www.mhspress.org

The Minnesota Historical Society Press is a member of the Association of American University Presses.

Manufactured in the United States of America

10 9 8 7 6 5 4 3 2 1

∞ The paper used in this publication meets the minimum requirements of the American National Standard for Information Sciences—Permanence for Printed Library Materials, ANSI Z39.48-1984.

International Standard Book Number
ISBN: 978-0-87351-892-5 (paper)

LIBRARY OF CONGRESS CATALOGING-IN-PUBLICATION DATA
Porter, Marie, 1979–
Sweet corn spectacular / Marie Porter.
    pages cm. — (The Northern plate)
Includes index.
ISBN 978-0-87351-892-5 (pbk. : alk. paper)
1. Cooking (Corn) I. Title.

TX809.M2P67 2013
641.6'315—dc23

                                                                2013006973

....

Sweet Corn Spectacular was designed and set in type by Cathy Spengler. The typefaces are Chaparral, TheSans, and Mandevilla.

Photography by Michael Porter, M. Porter Photography.

For my husband, The King of All Corn Freaks.

....

Contents

Sweet Corn Spectacular

Bacon-Wrapped Corn on the Cob >

Corn: The Basics

When I was a child, corn—sometimes canned, sometimes creamed, sometimes fresh on the cob—was an integral part of my family's diet. It was so ubiquitous that I never really gave much thought to it, if that makes any sense. As time passed, I came to appreciate the beauty of a perfect ear of fresh sweet corn. I grew up in Manitoba, where the Morden Corn and Apple Festival was a big deal—and the corn there was so much plumper and sweeter than anything that came frozen or in a can. Those golden ears of corn were something to look forward to throughout the year and then to gorge ourselves silly on when the time was right.

I eventually left my hometown and moved out east—and the corn was never the same. The sweetness of that prairie corn just wasn't there. Instead of fresh from the farm, the commonly available corn had been trucked in and had gone starchy. Who knew corn's quality could change so fast? It was back to canned and frozen for me.

Then I moved to Minnesota and married the King of All Corn Freaks.

Like me, he had been raised on corn. Canned corn was a regular part of his diet, and every summer his family made a point of picking up fresh corn from a roadside stand en route to the cabin. Unlike me, he was perfectly okay with making meals out of nothing but corn. If he had a can of creamed corn on hand, why would he need anything else? That was his bliss.

While I enjoyed corn, he could survive on it. Seriously. While many people will joke that they could live on a particular food, he really would be perfectly happy with nothing but corn-based meals for the rest of his life.

Early on in our relationship, I decided to put his love of corn to the test, and so began "The Day of Corn." For his birthday one year, all of his meals and snacks were corn based. We had corn pancakes for breakfast, corn salsa and corn chips as a snack, a cornmeal bake for lunch, corn burgers for supper—even corn ice cream for dessert. He loved it. So began a tradition in our household: coming up with all kinds of new and interesting ways to cook with corn—leading eventually to this book.

WHAT IS CORN?

Corn belongs to *Zea,* a genus of grasses in the family *poaceae.* Contrary to its popular home-cooking use as a vegetable, corn is a grain. Not just any grain, mind you: corn is known as America's first grain, having been cultivated over six thousand years ago.

Corn began in Mesoamerica as a domesticated variety of teosinte, an ancient grass. Popular cultivation spread from there, throughout a large portion of what is now North America as well as the northern parts of what is now South America. Sometime in the late fifteenth or early sixteenth century, corn made its way across the Atlantic Ocean, likely on Columbus's first or second trip home. Landing in Europe, it soon gained a foothold in northern Africa and Asia.

The earliest cultivars didn't look or taste anything like the corn of today: they had small kernels spaced farther apart and were far more starchy. Over thousands of years, corn has been cultivated to be larger, with plumper and more numerous kernels. Corn destined for eating as is, rather than being milled or otherwise processed, was developed to be much sweeter than earlier—or more industrial—counterparts.

Nowadays, corn is the most important and prolific crop grown in the United States, used for fuel and in some plastic production in addition to its role as a fresh food and processed grain product.

SELECTING, HANDLING, AND STORING CORN

Corn is a relatively finicky "vegetable," losing its oomph pretty quickly after being picked. Once corn is harvested, its sugars begin converting to starch. Along the way, the sweetness diminishes and the corn begins to taste mealy—not at all the tender, sweet kernels that you get from a fresher ear of corn.

Of course, corn should be eaten while it's as fresh as possible, but how do you determine what's "fresh"? Look for a pale green stem and for silk that is only just beginning to brown. Stems that are white or brown or even yellowed are past their prime. Ears should have fresh, healthy-looking husks—don't buy if the husks have dried out. Rather than being long and skinny, the ear should have a good-sized diameter. Upon peeling back the husk, you will want to see kernels that are fat and firm, shiny, and free of any bugs, mold, or rot.

When purchasing corn from the grocery store or farmers market, resist the urge to shuck it right on the spot. Leaving the husks on protects the corn and keeps it moist, preserving its freshness. Remember that corn will lose its sweetness very fast. Always try to use or preserve corn within a couple days of purchase. Wrap corn—still in its husk—in damp paper towels and refrigerate in a plastic bag.

Right before cooking your corn, you'll need to shuck it. Peel back the husk—the green, leafy portion of the corn—and snap off any remaining portion of the stalk. While the kernels, cob, and even the husk have their uses, you'll definitely want to get rid of the corn silk that clings to the cob. Use a damp paper towel to quickly and easily remove the threads—just wipe it down the ear in a straight-line motion, starting at the tip, heading toward the stalk.

COOKING WITH CORN

Before getting to all of the wonderful and crazy things you can make with corn, let's address the basic preparations. Sometimes you just want a perfectly cooked ear of corn on the cob.

BOILING Boiling is probably the most popular preparation of fresh corn on the cob, and for good reason: it is quick and easy and—when done right—produces really tasty results. The key to properly boiling corn is to not overcook it. Fresh corn kernels contain "milk," and when overcooked, this liquid firms up and the corn becomes tough. You're aiming more to just heat the corn rather than actually cook it.

For corn that is nice and fresh, bring a pot of water to a boil and then add shucked ears of corn. Allow to cook for 3 minutes and then drain.

For corn that may be a little past its prime, add a bit of milk—about ½ cup—to boiling water along with a couple tablespoons of sugar. This boost will help bring the corn back to a sweeter taste. Milk and sugar are not only unnecessary when preparing very fresh corn, they're undesirable: you don't want to mask the great flavor of perfectly fresh corn on the cob.

When boiling corn on the cob, never, ever salt the water. The salt toughens the kernel as it draws moisture from the corn. Not cool! You're free to salt the corn—whether by using salted butter or by sprinkling salt directly onto the cob—when you're ready to eat it.

STEAMING If you have a steamer, this technique is another attractive option for cooking corn. Simply cover the bottom of a steamer with a few inches of water and arrange shucked ears of corn on the steamer's rack. Steam for 5 to 10 minutes, or until just heated through.

MICROWAVING Some people enjoy microwaving their corn, preferring the ease and speed to all other methods. It's all good.

There are two main ways of nuking corn on the cob, both of which amount to a steaming method.

You can microwave the corn right in the husk. The husk holds in the moisture as the cob is heated, essentially steaming it right in its own casing. Place an unshucked cob in the microwave and heat it on high for 2 to 3 minutes.

Alternatively, you can steam shucked corn in a glass bowl. Add a couple inches of water to the bottom of a glass cooking dish and then arrange shucked ears of corn in the bowl. Cover with plastic wrap, cut a few slits in it, and microwave on high for 4 to 6 minutes. Once the time is up, *carefully* remove the plastic wrap: while the slits allow steam to escape, there will still be a fair amount of steam remaining in the bowl. Don't burn yourself.

OVEN ROASTING Cooking corn in the oven is a great way to impart a bit of a "roasty" flavor. Place corn—still in the husk—directly on the oven rack and roast for 30 minutes at 350 degrees. Much like microwaving, this method also steams the cob within its casing.

BACON-WRAPPED CORN ON THE COB

This is a simple way to prepare corn on the cob: there's not really anything elegant about it, but it's such a tasty side dish. The bacon adds flavor, salt, and fat to the corn as it roasts, basting the corn in wonderful deliciousness.

SERVES 4

8 strips bacon (regular, not thick cut)

4 ears fresh sweet corn, husks removed

pepper

salt, optional

Preheat broiler to high. Wrap 2 strips of bacon around each ear of corn, securing with toothpicks. Arrange on a broiling pan; sprinkle with pepper. Broil for 6 to 8 minutes. Remove pan from oven, flip cobs, and continue broiling for another 4 to 5 minutes or until bacon reaches desired doneness. Add salt to taste (if using; the bacon provides salt, so adding more is entirely optional). ◊

GRILLING Grilling has long been a favorite way of cooking food during the summer months, and it's a great way to prepare corn on the cob. Everyone seems to have their own favorite method. As it's largely a matter of preference, I highly encourage you to experiment and see what you like best. Here are a few techniques:

- Shuck the corn; grill over indirect heat for 8 to 10 minutes.
- Shuck the corn; heat in boiling water for 2 minutes, and then grill over direct heat just until grill marks form.
- Peel back the husk of the corn; remove corn silk. Apply butter to the cob and replace the husk to encase the butter. Grill for a few minutes over direct heat. If you like your corn a little charred, re-

Grilled corn

move a bit of the husk before grilling—but not enough to allow the butter to escape.

- Completely shuck the corn, dip it in water, and grill for a few minutes over direct heat.
- Soak toothpicks in water for at least 30 minutes. Wrap shucked corn in strips of bacon (1½–2 strips per cob); secure ends of bacon with soaked toothpicks. Grill until bacon is cooked.
- Soak shucked ears of corn in a mixture of half buttermilk, half water for an hour or two, and then grill over direct heat for a few minutes.

EAT IT RAW! If you're lucky enough to get your hands on some peak-season, perfectly fresh corn, try eating it raw. Not advisable for off-season or starchy corn.

SMOKING Have a smoker? You can use it for more than just meat: smoked corn on the cob is fabulous.

To smoke corn on the cob, first remove the corn silk. Pull the outer husk down but not all the way off the corn. Remove the silk and soak the ears in a bucket of cold water for at least an hour, preferably 2 or more. Meanwhile, prepare a fire in your smoker, using whatever flavor wood chips you like.

Using paper towels, pat dry the ears of corn, and then brush kernels with olive oil and replace the corn husk around the ear. Place cobs into the smoker, leaving space around each. Allow to smoke for 45 minutes or so, and then remove from smoker. Carefully peel back the husk of each cob of corn, brush ears with butter (try a compound butter, page 84), and replace the husk once more. Return cobs to the smoker and allow to smoke for another 30 to 45 minutes. Serve with more butter.

FREEZING Have you found yourself with more perfectly sweet, fresh corn on the cob than you can possibly eat in the next two days? Freeze some of it!

Get a large pot of water boiling, and remove the husks from the corn. Blanch whole cobs of corn at a full rolling boil for about 3 minutes. Then remove cobs from boiling water and immediately plunge into ice-cold water to stop the cooking process. Allow cobs to sit in the ice water for another 5 minutes, and then drain.

Use a sharp knife to cut the kernels from each cooled cob of corn, and spread kernels in a single layer on a cookie sheet lined with parchment paper. Freeze for 1 hour. (You can skip this step if you don't need the kernels individually frozen.) Place kernels into good-quality freezer bags or—better yet—vacuum-sealed bags. Remove as much air as you can, label with the date, and freeze. The corn is best used within three months but will keep for eight months.

A note on using frozen corn kernels for the recipes in this book: with corn being so seasonal, frozen corn can be an attractive alternative to no corn at all. To substitute frozen kernels in these recipes, know that 1 cob of corn is equal to about ⅔–¾ cup kernels. ◊

Breakfast Foods

S tart your day with fresh corn! The sweet taste and starch base of fresh sweet corn lends itself wonderfully to a variety of breakfast applications. Grains have always been a big part of a typical breakfast: why not incorporate corn into that tradition? It's easy to go beyond cornflakes—from the simple (fresh corn as cereal) to the sublime (stratas or soufflés).

Hot Fresh Corn "Cereal"

When I was young, one of my favorite breakfast foods was sliced bananas in milk, with sugar. It was incredibly simple, but so good. Now being married to the biggest corn freak in the world, I wanted to do a corn version for my husband. I tweaked it a bit to really focus on the best qualities of the corn. It's now a warm dish, with the sweetness incorporated into the liquid rather than sprinkled on top. The milk has been swapped out for coconut cream, making the dish seem more breakfast-y. A bit of cornstarch thickens the mixture, really driving home the feeling of comfort food.

Coconut cream, a creamy liquid, is usually sold in the Asian foods aisle. It is not to be confused with creamed coconut, which is much, much thicker.

SERVES 2

....

3–4 ears fresh sweet corn, husks removed

1 (18-ounce) can coconut cream

2 tablespoons granulated sugar

salt

1 tablespoon cornstarch

2 tablespoons water

....

> >

Using a sharp knife, carefully cut kernels off the ears of corn. Add kernels to a pot with coconut cream and sugar; heat until warm. Season with salt to taste. Whisk together the cornstarch and water until smooth. Add to pot of corn, stirring until well combined. Continue to heat until sauce thickens a bit, then remove from heat and serve. ◊

BREAKFAST CORN MUFFINS

Corn is such a versatile ingredient, the possibilities for these muffins are endless. See below for a few suggestions to get you started. **MAKES ABOUT 12 MUFFINS**

....

1½ cups all-purpose flour

¾ cup cornmeal

1 teaspoon baking powder

½ teaspoon salt

8 tablespoons (1 stick) butter, softened

⅔ cup granulated sugar

2 tablespoons honey

2 large eggs

⅔ cup milk

2 ears fresh sweet corn, husks removed

....

Preheat oven to 400 degrees. Prepare muffin pan with cupcake liners or grease well. Combine flour, cornmeal, baking powder, and salt, stirring until well combined. Set aside.

In a large bowl, beat together butter, sugar, and honey until light and fluffy. Add eggs and milk, stirring carefully until well incorporated. Mix in the dry ingredients, stirring just until combined. Using a sharp knife, carefully cut kernels off the ears of corn. Stir corn into batter, just until distributed.

Spoon batter into prepared muffin pan. Bake for 22 to 25 minutes, until a knife or toothpick inserted into the center of a muffin comes out clean.

Variations

- *Blueberry:* Add 1 cup fresh blueberries along with the corn kernels.
- *Peanut Butter and Banana:* Decrease sugar to ½ cup. Add ½ cup peanut butter when beating the butter and sugar mixture and 1 chopped banana with the corn kernels.
- *Jalapeño, Bacon, and Cheese:* Decrease sugar to ¼ cup. Add 1 finely chopped jalapeño, 6 crumbled slices crispy bacon, and 1 cup shredded sharp Cheddar cheese along with the corn kernels.
- *Sausage:* Decrease sugar to ¼ cup. Add 1 cup crumbled or sliced cooked breakfast sausage, ¼ cup finely chopped onion, and 1 cup shredded cheese along with the corn kernels.
- *Sour Cream and Onion:* Decrease sugar to ⅓ cup and milk to ¼ cup. Add ½ cup sour cream with the milk and eggs. Add ½ cup finely sliced green onions with the corn kernels. (This combination is also tasty with bacon.) ◊

Breakfast Corn Muffins

SWEET CORN PANCAKES

I created this recipe for my husband's first "day of corn" breakfast, and it was a huge hit. While many recipes use straight-up canned corn kernels, I wanted the corn flavor to permeate the batter itself. This recipe involves a little more effort than others, but it is well worth it. As with many pancake recipes, the batter also works well in a waffle maker. If you don't have buttermilk, use ¾ cup milk with 1½ teaspoons lemon juice mixed in. **MAKES ABOUT 4 SERVINGS**

3 ears fresh sweet corn, husks removed

¾ cup buttermilk (see head note)

2 large eggs

4 tablespoons (½ stick) butter, melted

1 cup all-purpose flour

2–3 tablespoons granulated sugar

1 tablespoon baking powder

½ teaspoon salt

optional toppings: maple syrup, whipped cream, blueberries

Using a sharp knife, carefully cut kernels off the ears of corn. Use the side of a fork to scrape any remaining corn kernel bits, milk, or pulp off the stripped cobs and into a blender. Add a large handful of the kernels to the blender, reserving the rest. Add buttermilk; blend until smooth. Add eggs and melted butter and blitz for a few seconds until well combined.

In a large bowl, stir together flour, sugar, baking powder, and salt. Add remaining corn kernels as well as the blended wet ingredients. Gently stir just until combined.

>>

Lightly oil a griddle or frying pan and preheat over medium or medium-low heat. Scoop ¼ cup portions of batter onto the griddle. Gently spread out batter into a larger circle, about 4 to 4½ inches in diameter. Cook until bubbles start popping through top surface. Flip pancakes and cook until nicely browned, and then remove to serving plate. Repeat with remaining batter. Serve with maple syrup, whipped cream, and/or blueberries if you like.

Variation: For a more savory pancake, decrease the sugar to 1–2 tablespoons and serve with salsa and sour cream. ◇

Basic Corn Buttermilk Scones

The sweetness of corn is a perfect complement to the flavor and texture of a traditional buttermilk biscuit. These scones work up quickly and easily, providing a wonderful base for a variety of both sweet and savory spreads. For a real treat, try with a peach-based jam. If you don't have buttermilk, use 1 cup milk with 1 tablespoon lemon juice mixed in. **SERVES 6**

2 cups all-purpose flour

½ cup cornmeal

2 teaspoons baking powder

1 teaspoon salt

6 tablespoons (¾ stick) butter, chilled and cut into small cubes

1 ear fresh sweet corn, husk removed

1 cup nonfat buttermilk (see head note)

Preheat oven to 400 degrees. Line baking sheet with parchment paper. In a large bowl, stir together flour, cornmeal, baking powder, and salt. Cut butter into dry ingredients using two forks or a pastry blender until butter is evenly distributed and mixture resembles gravel.

Using a sharp knife, carefully cut kernels off the ear of corn. Add kernels and buttermilk to dry ingredients and stir just until combined—mixture will be a little sticky.

Turn out dough onto a floured surface, sprinkling some flour on top. Gently knead for a few seconds, and then gather dough up into a ball. Press down to an even one-inch thickness and, using a sharp knife, cut the dough into 3½–inch squares and then in half to form triangles. Transfer scones to prepared baking sheet and bake for about 25 minutes or until golden brown.

Variations

- Add 1 cup shredded Cheddar cheese and 1–2 finely chopped jalapeños with the corn kernels.
- Add ⅔ cup fresh blueberries with the corn kernels.
- Add ⅔ cup sweetened dried cranberries with the corn kernels.
- Add zest of 1 orange with the corn kernels (also works well with dried cranberries). ◊

Sweet Corn Fritters—American Style

Frying makes everything better, doesn't it? Corn is no exception to this rule, and fritters are a great way to enjoy the fresh corn of late summer. Beyond breakfast, these also make a tasty snack or side dish later in the day. **SERVES 4**

vegetable oil for frying

1 cup all-purpose flour

1 teaspoon baking powder

1 tablespoon granulated sugar

½ teaspoon salt

¼ teaspoon cayenne, optional

2 large eggs

½ cup milk

3 ears fresh sweet corn, husks removed

1 cup add-ins (see page 23)

Heat 2–3 inches vegetable oil to 375 degrees in a pot or deep fryer. In a large bowl, mix flour, baking powder, sugar, salt, and cayenne (if using). In a separate bowl, whisk together eggs and milk until smooth. Pour milk and egg mixture into the dry ingredients, stirring well. Using a sharp knife, carefully cut kernels off the ears of corn. Mix kernels and add-ins into the batter until evenly coated.

Use an ice cream scoop or two spoons to carefully scoop small amounts (2 tablespoons or less) of batter into the preheated oil. Fry in small batches for a few minutes on each side, until fritters are golden brown. Use a slotted metal spoon to transfer cooked fritters to paper towel–lined plate. Serve hot.

Add-ins: Mix and match any of the following, in whatever proportions you prefer, about 1 cup total: chopped onions, red or green pepper, cilantro, parsley, or green onions. While vegetables are traditional, you can include some crispy, crumbled bacon if you like. Feel free to add seasonings to this base recipe: depending on your choice of add-ins, various dried herbs and spices will work well. ◇

SWEET CORN FRITTERS—COLOMBIAN STYLE

While the American fritter incorporates whole-kernel corn and other vegetables, the Colombian style uses a puree of fresh corn for a decidedly different type of fritter—and, bonus: this one is gluten free. **SERVES 4**

> vegetable oil for frying
> 3 ears fresh sweet corn, husks removed
> ½ cup shredded cheese (for a traditional approximation, try queso fresco)
> 2 large eggs
> ¼ cup granulated sugar
> 1 teaspoon baking powder
> ½ teaspoon salt

Heat 2–3 inches vegetable oil to 350 degrees in a pot or deep fryer. Using a sharp knife, carefully cut kernels off the ears of corn. Place kernels in bowl of a food processor and process until finely chopped. Add cheese, eggs, sugar, baking powder, and salt and process until smooth and well combined.

Use an ice cream scoop or two spoons to carefully scoop small amounts (less than a tablespoon) of batter into the preheated oil. Fry in small batches for a couple of minutes on each side, until fritters are golden brown. Use a slotted metal spoon to transfer cooked fritters to paper towel–lined plate. Serve hot. ◇

Easy Corn Soufflé

Soufflé is a dish that many people don't understand. Either it's this big scary thing, or it's instant cornbread with stuff thrown into it. Never fear: here is a recipe that produces a traditional soufflé using easy techniques. Yes, the soufflé will fall about 45 seconds after you take it out of the oven— that's just thermodynamics, not a failing on the part of the cook! **SERVES 4**

butter

3 ears fresh sweet corn, husks removed

7 large eggs

½ cup sour cream

¼ cup milk

¼ cup cornmeal

½–1 teaspoon dry mustard

¼ teaspoon cayenne

½ teaspoon salt

¾ cup shredded Swiss cheese

¼ cup shredded Parmesan cheese

6 strips crispy cooked bacon, crumbled, optional

Preheat oven to 375 degrees. Use butter to grease soufflé ramekins: you'll need two 16-ounce or four 8-ounce ceramic ramekins, about 3 inches tall.

Using a sharp knife, carefully cut kernels off the ears of corn. Place kernels in bowl of a food processor and process until finely chopped. Add eggs, sour cream, milk, cornmeal, dry mustard, cayenne, and salt, and blitz for 30 seconds. Stir in cheeses and bacon (if using). Pour into prepared ramekins and bake for 50 minutes (if using 16-ounce ramekins) or 35 minutes (if using 8-ounce ramekins). Serve immediately. ◊

Easy Corn Soufflé

CORN FRITTATA

The beauty of frittatas is that you can add just about anything to them. This recipe is for a very basic version of a corn frittata. Dress it up by mixing in bacon, vegetables, your choice of herbs and spices, whatever you have on hand. SERVES 4–6

....

8 large eggs

¼ cup milk

1–2 cloves garlic, pressed or minced

2–3 ears fresh sweet corn, husks removed

1 small onion, finely chopped

2 cups add-ins (see page 27)

2 tablespoons olive oil, divided

salt and pepper

½–1 cup shredded cheese

....

Preheat oven to 450 degrees. In a large bowl, whisk together eggs, milk, and garlic. Set aside.

Using a sharp knife, carefully cut kernels off the ears of corn. Add kernels to a large, ovenproof skillet along with onion, raw add-ins, and 1 tablespoon olive oil. Cook over medium-high heat, stirring, until onions—and add-ins, as applicable—are tender. Season with salt and pepper to taste. Remove from heat and allow mixture to cool slightly.

Pour cooled mixture into the egg mixture along with the cheese and any additional add-ins, stirring to coat. Wipe out skillet and add remaining tablespoon olive oil. Pour egg and vegetable mixture into the skillet and cook over medium heat for 2 minutes without stirring. Reduce heat to low, cover pan, and continue to cook for another 2 minutes. Remove lid and transfer skillet to top shelf of oven. Bake until entire frittata is set and the top is golden brown, about 10 minutes. Cut into wedges and serve warm.

Add-ins: Mix and match any of the following, in whatever proportions you like: chopped, cooked red or green pepper; chopped zucchini, mushrooms, broccoli, cilantro, parsley, or green onions; fresh basil; chopped cooked potatoes; chopped cooked chicken; breakfast sausage chunks; bacon. (I tend to add vegetables and meats in approximately equal proportions if using chicken, less meat if using sausage or bacon.) Feel free to add seasonings to this base recipe: depending on your choice of add-ins, various dried herbs and spices will work well. ◊

SWEET CORN QUICHE

Writing a traditional quiche recipe is a challenge—like many other dishes in this book, it's the kind of thing I never make the same way twice. How do I narrow down which ingredients I want to recommend?

Here is a winning combination of flavors for a corn quiche. Feel free to play with it, swapping out the meats, vegetables, and cheeses with other types if you so desire. **SERVES 6**

....

2 ears fresh sweet corn, husks removed

1 cup milk

½ small onion

4 large eggs

½ teaspoon salt

1 cup cubed smoked ham

¼ cup finely chopped green bell pepper

¾ cup shredded Swiss cheese, divided

1 (9-inch) deep-dish piecrust
(if crust is frozen, thaw before using)

....

>>

Preheat oven to 375 degrees. Using a sharp knife, carefully cut kernels off the ears of corn. Process kernels and milk together in a food processor or blender until smooth. Add onion, eggs, and salt and blitz a few seconds, until onion is finely chopped. Sprinkle ham, green pepper, and ½ cup cheese over the empty piecrust; pour filling over top.

Bake 40 minutes. Sprinkle remaining ¼ cup cheese on top and continue baking until quiche is puffy and fully set, another 10 minutes or so. Serve warm.

Variation: Feel free to swap out the veggies, cheese, and meats. Goat cheese, red pepper, and asparagus, for instance, is an amazing combination. ◇

CORN, KALE, AND BACON STRATA

This is my favorite flavor combination for a breakfast strata, but it's definitely open to tinkering and interpretation. Stratas are easy to adapt and a great way to use up whatever odds and ends you may have in the fridge. Swap out the kale for spinach or for a cup or so of your favorite veggie. Use any kind of cheese; add herbs and spices if you'd like.

I like to use crusty, day-old baguette to make the strata, but it can also work with your favorite sourdough, French, Italian, or random artisan-type breads—just leave them out to dry a bit overnight and cut into 1-inch cubes. You'll want about 8 cups of bread cubes, whatever type you use.
SERVES 6–8

- 2 ears fresh sweet corn, husks removed
- 1 large onion, finely chopped
- 6 strips bacon, chopped
- 1 bunch kale, chopped (about 4–5 cups)

½ teaspoon salt, divided

½ teaspoon pepper, divided

9 large eggs

1–2 tablespoons Dijon mustard

2⅔ cups milk

1 baguette, cut into 1-inch cubes (about 8 cups; see head note)

2½ cups shredded Swiss, Gruyère, or Jarlsberg cheese

....

Using a sharp knife, carefully cut kernels off the ears of corn. In a large skillet over medium heat, cook onion and bacon together until onion is tender and bacon is cooked but not crispy. Add kale and cook, stirring, until kale is wilted. Stir in corn; season with a bit of salt and pepper. Continue cooking mixture, stirring, for 1 more minute, and then remove from heat.

In a medium mixing bowl, whisk together eggs and mustard. Add milk and remaining salt and pepper, and continue whisking until well combined. Use cooking spray or butter to grease a 9x13–inch baking dish. Arrange half of the bread cubes evenly in the pan; top with half of the kale mixture, then half of the cheese. Repeat layering one more time, ending with cheese on top. Pour egg mixture evenly over everything, wrap dish with plastic wrap, and chill for at least 2 hours or overnight.

About an hour and a half before serving, remove strata from fridge and preheat oven to 350 degrees. Let strata sit on the counter for 20 or so minutes to take off the chill. Remove plastic wrap from strata and bake for 45 to 50 minutes. Strata is ready when it is cooked through and golden brown on top. Serve hot. ◊

Corn, Kale, and Bacon Strata

"Corned" Beef Hash

What started out as an attempt at being "punny" actually produced a very balanced, delicious breakfast. The sweetness of the corn is the perfect complement to the saltiness of the corned beef. This dish goes particularly well with a fried egg on top. **SERVES 4–6**

1 pound red potatoes, cut into ½-inch cubes

2 tablespoons olive oil

1 large green bell pepper, chopped

1 large onion, chopped

2 ears fresh sweet corn, husks removed

1 pound cooked corned beef brisket, shredded or chopped

¼ cup chopped parsley

salt and pepper

Boil potatoes until just tender. Drain well; set aside. In a large skillet over medium heat, warm olive oil and cook green pepper and onion, stirring, until vegetables are tender. Add potatoes; continue to cook until potatoes are browned.

Using a sharp knife, carefully cut kernels off the ears of corn. Add kernels to pan along with corned beef. Continue cooking until corned beef is heated through. Add parsley, stir well, and season with salt and pepper to taste. Serve hot. ◊

Roasted Corn and Pepper Hash with Ham and Eggs

This recipe is great done as leftovers after a grilled dinner. Toss an extra couple ears of corn and the peppers and onion on the grill along with supper one night, and then use them the next morning. **SERVES 4**

....

1 red bell pepper

1 poblano chile

1 small red onion

2 ears fresh sweet corn, husks removed

¼ cup olive oil

1 tablespoon butter

2 cups diced smoked ham (hickory works well)

1 clove garlic, pressed or minced

salt and pepper

4 large eggs

....

Slice red pepper and poblano chile into large flat pieces and onion into ½-inch-thick slices. Brush vegetables and corncobs with olive oil. Grill everything until as "done" as you would like—personally, I like some dark grill marks but not an overall char. Remove items as they are ready: the pepper and chile will cook the fastest. When cool enough to handle, chop vegetables and use a sharp knife to remove kernels from the corn; set aside.

Heat butter in a large skillet; add ham and garlic. Cook over medium heat for 2 minutes, until ham is warmed through. Add chopped vegetables and corn. Stir well, and season with salt and pepper to taste.

Arrange four "wells" in the skillet ingredients. Crack an egg into each, cover pan, and cook until eggs reach desired doneness, about 2 to 3 minutes for runny yolks or 4 to 6 minutes for hard yolks. Serve hot. ◊

Appetizers & Side Dishes

ppetizers and side dishes have traditionally been the stage on which fresh corn is featured, but you needn't stop at boiled or grilled corn on the cob. Expand your repertoire of corn-based side dishes with recipes ranging from deep-fried goodies to cornbreads to salads to creamed corn to dips and more.

PARCHED CORN

Parched corn is a very traditional "trail food," used as a high-energy, light-weight comestible by Native Americans. And it was probably the predecessor to modern-day corn nuts.

whole ears fresh sweet corn, husks removed

olive oil

salt and seasonings (see below)

Preheat oven to 260 degrees. Using a sharp knife, carefully cut kernels off the ears of corn. Working in batches of about 1 cup at a time, heat the kernels in a skillet set over medium to medium-high heat, stirring every minute or so. As the moisture in the kernels evaporates, the corn becomes "parched."

After about 5 minutes, add a little oil—about 2 to 2½ teaspoons—to the corn, tossing to coat well. Add seasonings, once again tossing to coat well. Spread out kernels in a single layer on a large cookie sheet lined with parchment paper, and roast in the oven for about 15 minutes. Allow to cool fully before serving or storing.

Seasonings: Try your favorite dry herbs and spices or even prepared popcorn seasonings (not the healthiest option, but they certainly taste good). Try chili powder, cumin, garlic salt, ground ginger, onion salt, paprika, red pepper flakes, seasoned salt, even brown sugar. ✧

HOMEMADE POPCORN

Okay, I'll admit it: this is one of those recipes that is probably more effort than it's reasonably worth—but there is something to be said for the "cool factor" involved in turning a cob of corn into popcorn. Some kind of bragging rights, at the very least.

fresh sweet corn, husks removed

To air dry: place corn into a cheesecloth or mesh bag and hang in a dry area of your home for about a week. To oven dry: heat oven to 200 degrees. Place whole ears of corn on a cookie sheet and set in the oven with the door held ajar (with a wooden spoon, for example). Allow to dry for about 8 hours. Whichever method you use, the key is to dry the corn kernels to 13–15 percent moisture. It's a matter of trial and error: when you think the corn has dried long enough, try popping a few kernels. If they pop properly, you're good to go.

Use a sharp knife to strip the dried kernels from the cobs. Use vegetable oil or a popcorn machine to pop the kernels as you normally would. For great flavor, use bacon grease in place of the oil.

For microwave popcorn: Place one cob worth of dried kernels into a paper bag. Fold the end of the bag over twice, bending the corners back to secure it shut. Microwave on high for about 3 minutes, until the pops are 2 to 3 seconds apart. Enjoy. ◇

ROASTED CORN AND PEPPER SALSA

This salsa, more "warm" than "hot," features a wonderful roasty flavor. Slightly more labor intensive than a fresh salsa, but very much worth it.

MAKES ABOUT 4 CUPS

....

- 2 red bell peppers
- 1 poblano chile
- 1 large onion
- 1–2 jalapeños
- 4 ears fresh sweet corn, husks removed
- ¼ cup olive oil
- 2–3 chipotles in adobo sauce, finely chopped
- 2 tablespoons adobo sauce
- 1 clove garlic, pressed or minced
- salt and pepper

....

Prepare grill. Slice red pepper and poblano chile into large flat pieces and onion into ½-inch-thick slices. Cut jalapeño(s) in half, removing ribs and seeds if you prefer a milder salsa. Brush vegetables and corn with olive oil. Grill everything until as "done" as you like (I prefer some dark grill marks but not an overall char). Remove items from the grill as they are ready—the pepper and chiles will cook the fastest. Allow everything to cool.

Chop the vegetables and place in a bowl. Use a sharp knife to remove kernels from the corn; add to the bowl and stir well. Add chopped chipotles, adobo sauce, and pressed garlic. Stir well, and season with salt and pepper to taste. Serve immediately, or cover and refrigerate for a day or so to let the flavors meld. ◊

Roasted Corn and Pepper Salsa

FRESH CORN SALSA

I modeled this recipe around the corn salsa at Chipotle restaurants, and it's a great multipurpose condiment: use it in salads, on grilled meats, in a burrito, or just as a dip. Remove ribs and seeds from the jalapeño for a milder salsa, if desired. **MAKES ABOUT 4½ CUPS**

- 4 ears fresh sweet corn, husks removed
- 1 small red onion, chopped
- 1–2 jalapeños, chopped (see head note)
- ½–⅔ cup chopped fresh cilantro
- ½ cup fresh lime juice (from about 3–4 limes)
- 1 clove garlic, pressed or minced, optional
- salt and pepper

Use a sharp knife to remove kernels from the corn; place in a large bowl. Add onion, jalapeño(s), and cilantro along with lime juice and garlic (if using). Stir well; season with salt and pepper to taste. ◇

Beer-Battered Corn on the Cob

A few years ago, I was particularly not in the mood to brave the crowds at the Minnesota State Fair, so I made my husband a deal. I would come up with a recipe for corn on the cob in a corn-based batter and deep-fry it IF we didn't go to the fair. Heck, I'd even do it "on a stick" to give him a bit more of the state fair experience if that's what it took. I lived up to my end of the bargain, and we were both pleasantly surprised by the results. Here's how you can make the same at home. SERVES 4

vegetable oil for frying

4 ears fresh sweet corn, husks removed

wooden "candy apple" skewers, optional

1 cup all-purpose flour

1 cup yellow cornmeal

1 teaspoon baking powder

1 teaspoon salt

1 large egg, beaten

1 (12-ounce) bottle beer

Dijon mustard or other dipping sauce

Preheat deep fryer to 375 degrees. If your deep fryer is small, cut each ear of corn in half crosswise. If using sticks, carefully push the sharp end of a stick into each ear of corn, far enough to be secure. Set aside.

In a bowl large enough to fit the ears of corn, mix together flour, cornmeal, baking powder, and salt. Add egg and beer; whisk until smooth. Dip corn ears in batter one at a time, turning until coated. Carefully place in deep fryer and fry for 2 to 4 minutes, until coating is as dark as you like it. Remove from fryer and set on paper towel–lined plate. Serve with Dijon mustard or dipping sauce of your choice. ◇

SCALLOPED CORN

This is a first for me: publishing someone else's recipe. My good friend Carrie insisted that her recipe is so addictive it must be included in this book, so here it is.

As the story goes, Carrie's former mother-in-law was a very nice person but not a creative cook. One thing she was known for, however, was a scalloped corn dish based on a magazine-clipped recipe involving canned corn. While everyone else raved, Carrie was less than impressed. Unable to resist an opportunity to show someone up (there's a reason we're friends), she quietly created her own version. She has not, however, served it to said former mother-in-law. **SERVES 8–10**

- 10 ears fresh sweet corn, husks removed
- 1 cup heavy cream
- 8 tablespoons (1 stick) butter, melted
- 3 large eggs, beaten well
- 2 cups crushed buttery crackers, divided
- 2 cups shredded Parmesan cheese, divided
- salt and pepper

Preheat oven to 350 degrees. Use a sharp knife to remove kernels from the corn. Transfer kernels to a large mixing bowl along with cream, melted butter, and beaten eggs. Stir in 1 cup crushed crackers and 1 cup Parmesan cheese. Season with salt and pepper to taste.

Pour corn mixture into a 9x13–inch baking dish and top with remaining cheese and cracker pieces. Bake for 30 minutes or until top is golden brown and inside is fluffy. Serve. ◊

SOUTHWEST FONDUE

Accompanied by cubes of bread, chunks of vegetables, and slices of fruit, this fondue makes a wonderful appetizer. Not in the mood for such a formal service? Set it out with tortilla chips as a hot cheese dip. **SERVES 4**

- 2 ears fresh sweet corn, husks removed
- 1 cup Mexican beer (Corona)
- 3 tablespoons fresh lime juice
- 1 red bell pepper, seeded and chopped
- 1 yellow bell pepper, seeded and chopped
- 1 orange bell pepper, seeded and chopped
- 1 jalapeño, seeded and chopped
- 1 fresno chile, seeded and chopped
- 1 habanero, seeded and chopped
- 6 cloves garlic, peeled and chopped
- 1 small onion
- 1½ pounds sharp Cheddar cheese, shredded (about 6 cups)
- 4 teaspoons cornstarch
- items for dipping: bread cubes, tortilla chips, blanched vegetables, sliced fruit

Use a sharp knife to remove kernels from the corn; set aside. In a medium saucepan, heat beer and lime juice over medium-low heat.

Place peppers, chiles, garlic, and onion in food processor or blender and process until finely chopped. Add vegetable mixture to the beer, increase heat to medium or medium-high, and cook until everything is soft and onion is translucent, about 5 minutes. Add corn; cook for 1 more minute.

>>

In a large bowl, toss shredded cheese with cornstarch. Add a good-sized handful to the pot, and stir until the cheese is completely melted in. Add another big handful and repeat until all the cheese is added, completely melted, and smooth (aside from the pepper bits, of course). Transfer to fondue pot if desired, and serve with cubes of bread; tortilla chips; blanched broccoli, cauliflower, and asparagus; or slices of apples and pears. ◊

Sweet Corn Bruschetta

This recipe is simple, elegant, and easy to tinker with. It's beautiful and delicious with the simplest of balsamic vinegars, but it is mind-blowingly amazing if you can get your hands on peach balsamic vinegar. **SERVES 4–6**

- 4 ears fresh sweet corn, husks removed
- 1 tablespoon honey
- 1 tablespoon granulated sugar
- 3 tablespoons balsamic vinegar (see head note)
- ¼ cup fresh basil leaves, cut into wide strips
- salt and pepper
- 1 baguette, cut into ¼- to ½-inch slices
- scant ¼ cup olive oil
- 4 ounces goat cheese

Preheat broiler. Using a sharp knife, carefully cut kernels off the ears of corn. In a large bowl, combine kernels, honey, sugar, and balsamic vinegar, tossing to coat. Stir in basil, and season with salt and pepper to taste. Brush both sides of each bread slice with olive oil, and arrange on a broiling pan.

\>\>

Sweet Corn Bruschetta

Broil bread slices for 3 minutes, flip them over, and broil for another 2 minutes, until golden. Remove from oven, spread each slice with goat cheese, and top with corn mixture. Serve immediately.

Variations

- Add diced fresh tomato to corn mixture.
- Add a little finely chopped onion to corn mixture.
- Add red pepper flakes for a bit of a kick.
- Swap basil for different fresh herbs—dill, tarragon, parsley, thyme, mint, cilantro.
- Add a pressed or minced garlic clove to corn mixture.
- Swap the goat cheese for mascarpone or cream cheese. ◊

ROASTED CORN AND POTATO SALAD

When I created this recipe, I intended it to be a roasted take on a traditional—cold!—potato salad. But as soon as the dressing was tossed on the hot potato salad, we couldn't help ourselves: we were picking at it long before it had a chance to cool. Oh, it was amazing—I think I actually preferred it hot to its later, chilled incarnation. SERVES 4–6

    1 pound bacon, chopped
    3 pounds red potatoes, cut into ¾- to 1-inch chunks
    salt and pepper
3–4 ears grilled fresh sweet corn (see page 10)
    4 ribs celery, sliced (about 2 cups)
    1 medium red onion, chopped
1–2 tablespoons finely chopped green onions

½ cup olive oil

⅓ cup apple cider vinegar

1 tablespoon Dijon mustard

2 cloves garlic, pressed or minced

....

Preheat oven to 400 degrees. Cook bacon until crispy; use a slotted spoon to remove bacon from pan and set it aside. Toss potato chunks with bacon drippings. Spread onto a baking sheet lined with parchment paper or foil; season with salt and pepper. Roast until fork tender, about 30 to 35 minutes.

While potatoes are roasting, use a sharp knife to carefully cut kernels off the ears of corn. In a large bowl, toss kernels, celery, red onion, green onions, and cooked bacon. Set aside. Whisk together olive oil, apple cider vinegar, mustard, garlic, and ½ teaspoon pepper until emulsified. Season with salt to taste.

When potatoes are ready, mix them into the large bowl of vegetables. Pour vinaigrette over top, tossing to coat. Serve immediately, allow to cool slightly and serve warm, or chill for later service. ◊

Cool Corn Dip

Cool Corn Dip

This recipe comes together quickly and is a huge hit at any party. **MAKES ABOUT 6 CUPS**

- 3 ears fresh sweet corn, husks removed
- 1 green bell pepper
- 1 red bell pepper
- 1 or more jalapeños
- 1–2 cloves garlic, pressed or minced
- 3 green onions, thinly sliced
- 2 cups shredded Monterey Jack cheese
- ½ teaspoon pepper
- ½ teaspoon salt
- 1 tablespoon fresh lime juice
- ⅔ cup mayonnaise
- 1 cup sour cream
- corn chips

Using a sharp knife, carefully cut kernels off the ears of corn; place in a large mixing bowl. Place peppers, chile, and garlic in bowl of a food processor and process until finely chopped. Add chopped mixture, green onions, and cheese to mixing bowl with corn; stir to combine. Add pepper, salt, and lime juice, tossing to coat. Add mayonnaise and sour cream, and stir until well combined. Cover bowl with plastic wrap, and chill for at least an hour to allow flavors to meld. Serve with corn chips.

Variation: Add ½ cup or more chopped fresh cilantro plus ½ teaspoon cumin for great Tex-Mex flavor. ◊

Hot and Cheesy Bacon Corn Dip

Bacon makes everything better, doesn't it? This dip is thick, rich, melty, and satisfying. While intended as a group-sized appetizer, I'll confess— two people can snarf this down as a very guilty meal. **MAKES 6–7 CUPS**

....

    3 ears fresh sweet corn, husks removed
    8 strips bacon, chopped
    1 medium onion, finely chopped
    4 ribs celery, finely chopped
    2 cloves garlic, pressed or minced
  ½ cup mayonnaise
    2 cups shredded Monterey Jack cheese
  salt and pepper
½–1 cup shredded mild or medium Cheddar cheese
  green onions, thinly sliced, optional
  corn chips

....

Preheat oven to 350 degrees. Using a sharp knife, carefully cut kernels off the ears of corn; set aside. In a large skillet over medium heat, fry bacon until cooked but not yet crispy. Add onion, celery, and garlic, and cook, stirring, until vegetables are tender. Add corn kernels and cook for 1 more minute. Remove from heat.

Add mayonnaise and Monterey Jack cheese to hot bacon mixture, stirring until well combined. Season with salt and pepper to taste. Transfer mixture to a greased 9x13–inch baking dish; top with Cheddar cheese. Bake, uncovered, for 20 minutes or until heated through and bubbly. Sprinkle hot dip with green onions; serve with corn chips.

Rather than baking in the oven, this dish can be heated through—and kept warm—in a slow cooker. Cook on high for 45 to 60 minutes. Once thoroughly heated, reduce heat to low.

Variation: Add 1–2 finely chopped jalapeños with the onion and celery. ◊

Esquites

Esquites is a creamy corn salad that is very popular in Mexico, where it's commonly sold by street vendors. The salad hits the perfect balance of sweet-salty and creamy-solid. **SERVES 4**

- 4 ears fresh sweet corn, husks removed
- 1 jalapeño or serrano chile, minced
- 1 clove garlic, pressed or minced
- ¼ cup mayonnaise
- 4 tablespoons (½ stick) butter, at room temperature
- 1 tablespoon fresh lime juice
- 2 green onions, thinly sliced
- ¼ cup chopped fresh cilantro
- ¼ teaspoon cayenne
- ⅓ cup crumbled queso fresco
- salt

Use a sharp knife to remove kernels from the corn; place kernels in a large pan along with jalapeño or serrano chile and garlic. Cook over medium heat, stirring frequently, until corn is roasty and heated through. Remove from heat.

As corn is cooking, prepare dressing. In a large mixing bowl, mix together mayonnaise and butter. Add lime juice, green onions, cilantro, and cayenne, stirring well to combine.

Once corn is cooked, transfer hot kernels to the mixing bowl, tossing to coat. Stir in queso fresco, and season with salt to taste. Divide mixture into 4 bowls or cups, and serve immediately. ◊

CORN, EDAMAME, AND RED PEPPER SALAD

My husband came home from a meeting one day with a little tub of left-over edamame salad. He'd never had it before, and he thought I would like it. That's what he claims, anyway. The real story is that he wanted me to replicate it because HE loved it so much. So here it is. **SERVES 4–6**

....

3	ears fresh sweet corn, husks removed
1	(16-ounce) bag frozen shelled edamame
1–2	red bell peppers, chopped
½	medium red onion, chopped
¼–½	cup chopped fresh cilantro
2	tablespoons fresh lime juice
1	tablespoon olive oil
1	clove garlic, pressed or minced
	salt and pepper

....

Use a sharp knife to remove kernels from the corn; set aside. Cook edamame according to package directions. In the last minute or two, add corn kernels. Once cooked, remove from heat, drain, and allow to cool. Place corn and edamame in a large mixing bowl along with red peppers, onion, and cilantro. Stir to combine.

In a small mixing bowl or measuring cup, combine lime juice, olive oil, and garlic; whisk to emulsify. Pour over salad, tossing to coat. Season with salt and pepper to taste. Cover salad with plastic wrap, and chill for at least 1 hour to allow flavors to combine. Toss one more time, and serve cold.

Variations: This combination is also great with a chopped avocado or two mixed in immediately before serving. Or add halved cherry tomatoes if you choose. ◇

Roasted Cornbread

I love this updated version of traditional cornbread—the roasted flavor from the corn and jalapeños really elevates it to something special. For extra roasty flavor, substitute blue cornmeal for regular yellow cornmeal. If you don't have buttermilk, use 1½ cups milk with 1 tablespoon lemon juice mixed in. **SERVES 12**

2–3 large jalapeños

3 ears fresh sweet corn, husks removed

¼ cup olive oil

12 tablespoons (1½ sticks) butter, softened

1 cup granulated sugar

3 large eggs

1½ cups buttermilk (see head note)

1½ cups all-purpose flour

1½ cups cornmeal (see head note)

1 teaspoon baking soda

1 teaspoon salt

Prepare grill. Preheat oven to 375 degrees, and grease a 9x13–inch baking dish with cooking spray, butter, or shortening.

Cut jalapeños in half, removing ribs and seeds if you prefer a milder bread. Brush jalapeños and corncobs with olive oil. Grill corn and jalapeños until as "done" as you like (I prefer some dark grill marks but not an overall char). Remove items as they are ready: the jalapeños will cook the fastest. Allow everything to cool. Chop the jalapeños, and use a sharp knife to remove kernels from the corn; set aside.

In a large bowl, beat butter and sugar until light and fluffy. Add in eggs and buttermilk, stirring until well incorporated. In a separate bowl, mix together flour, cornmeal, baking soda, and salt, stirring until well combined. Mix the dry ingredients into the wet ingredients, stirring just until combined. Stir corn and jalapeños into batter just until distributed. Spread batter into prepared pan. Bake for 35 to 40 minutes, until a knife or toothpick inserted into the center of the bread comes out clean.

Variations

- Add 1 cup of shredded cheese when you stir in the corn. Try smoked provolone.

- Add 1 or more tablespoons adobo sauce to the batter for an added smoky kick. ◇

CREAMED CORN

Why go for canned corn when you can load it up with cream cheese, butter, and MORE cheese? Sinful, yes, but oh so worth it. SERVES 6–8

6 ears fresh sweet corn, husks removed

1 cup heavy cream

1 tablespoon granulated sugar

4 ounces cream cheese, softened

3 tablespoons butter

⅓ cup grated Parmesan cheese

salt

Use a sharp knife to remove kernels from the corn. Place kernels in a medium pot along with heavy cream and sugar. Bring to a boil, reduce heat, and simmer for 5 minutes. Add in cream cheese and butter, stirring until everything is well incorporated. Simmer for 5 more minutes. Add Parmesan cheese, stirring until melted and mixed in. Season with salt to taste, and serve hot. ◇

Spicy Corn Pakoras

Pakoras are surprisingly easy to make, and the warmth of the Indian spices pairs well with the sweetness of the corn. **SERVES 4**

....

vegetable oil for deep frying

1¼ cups garbanzo flour

¼ cup white rice flour

2 teaspoons salt

2 teaspoons hot curry powder

1 teaspoon cumin

¼ teaspoon baking powder

1 cup water

3 ears fresh sweet corn, husks removed

1 cup peeled, finely chopped yam or sweet potato

1 cup finely chopped onion

1–2 jalapeños, finely chopped

½ cup chopped fresh cilantro

Cilantro Mint Chutney (recipe follows)

....

Heat 2 to 3 inches vegetable oil to 375 degrees in a pot or deep fryer. In a large bowl, stir together flours, salt, spices, and baking powder. Add water and stir well to form a thick batter. Allow batter to sit for 5 minutes or so, to soften the flour.

Use a sharp knife to remove kernels from the corn. Mix kernels into batter along with yam, onion, jalapeño, and cilantro. Stir well until everything is evenly coated with batter.

Use an ice cream scoop or two spoons to carefully scoop small amounts (¼ cup or less) of batter into the preheated oil. Fry for a few minutes on each side, until patties are golden brown. Use a slotted metal spoon to transfer cooked patties to a paper towel–lined plate. Serve hot, with Cilantro Mint Chutney.

CILANTRO MINT CHUTNEY

This chutney comes together very quickly and is a perfect accompaniment not only to the pakoras but also to roasted corn on the cob.

MAKES ABOUT 1 CUP

....

2 bunches fresh cilantro

2 bunches fresh mint leaves (about half the volume of the cilantro)

1 jalapeño, chopped

juice of ½ large lime (about 1 tablespoon)

½ teaspoon salt

1 teaspoon cumin

1 teaspoon granulated sugar

....

Measure everything but the cilantro into a food processor, and pulse until finely chopped and the texture is nearly a paste. Add a handful of cilantro, and pulse until combined. Add the rest of the cilantro, and pulse until well chopped and combined. Cover and refrigerate until ready to use. ◊

Main Dishes

hile traditionally set alongside the main dish of any given meal, corn isn't merely a side dish: it can be the star of the show. Recipes in this chapter highlight corn as the main attraction in chowders, chili, casseroles, and more.

Low Country Boil (aka Frogmore Stew)

This southern dish can be done so many ways, the possibilities truly are endless. It can be a quick and easy meal for two or the basis for a GREAT cookout party with friends. It can be a frugal, thrifty dinner or as extravagant a feast as you want.

The main ingredients are basic: corn, smoked sausage, potatoes, shrimp, lemons, seasoning. Bring a big pot of seasoned water to boiling, and one by one add the ingredients to the pot, starting with potatoes (which take the longest to cook) and ending with shrimp (which take very little time to cook).

Of course, I never do anything the way you're supposed to—and, besides, I'm not even southern, which means I'm exempt from any rules that might be applied here, right? The big change I like to make is with the seasoning. Old Bay Seasoning is traditionally used. Not only is that choice boring, but the salt content is insane, and, really, isn't customization always more fun? I flavor the broth with a mix of fresh (onions, garlic, green onions, jalapeños, etc.) and dried (sage, pepper, dry mustard, bay leaves, etc.) ingredients. You can also start your broth in different ways: use some chicken broth or boil fresh shrimp shells for added flavor—just remove the shells before tossing in food and other seasonings. Or add a can or two of beer to the broth for enhanced flavor. Any of these is a much better option than just water and Old Bay Seasoning, in my not-so-humble opinion.

>>

The ingredients are also customizable. Corn, potatoes, shrimp, and sausage make a solid foundation, but feel free to add clams, mussels, even crab legs. It's your stew.

Now that the whole thing sounds way more complicated than it is, I'll give you a basic recipe and let you have at it. This makes a substantial amount of food, so don't be surprised if you have leftovers. But it also makes ridiculously good food, so don't be surprised if you don't have leftovers because everyone gorged themselves. That's called success!

....

BROTH

For every 3 people being served:

  1 onion, quartered

  1 lemon, quartered

  about 1 can beer, optional, as much or as little as you want

  chicken broth, optional, as much or as little as you want

  garlic, as much as you want

2–3 green onions, chopped, optional

2–3 jalapeños, habaneros, or other hot chiles, chopped, optional

  1 teaspoon dried sage

  pepper, as much as you like

  dry mustard, as much as you like

1–2 bay leaves

  handful chopped fresh parsley

MAIN INGREDIENTS

Per person:

⅓ pound red potatoes, halved or quartered

½ pound smoked sausage (kielbasa), cut into 2- to 3-inch pieces

1–2 ears fresh sweet corn, husks removed, cut into 3-inch pieces

⅓ pound uncooked shrimp

whatever else you want: clams, crab, mussels, etc.

cocktail sauce, optional

Dijon mustard, optional

....

Get a pot of an appropriate size for the amount of food you're planning to cook. The more people being served, the bigger the pot. Fill it about ⅓ full with water. Add whatever ingredients from the broth list that you plan to use, plus other ingredients of your choice for flavor. Bring to a boil.

Add potatoes and sausage, plus more water if necessary. Sausage doesn't take long to cook, but it will add flavor to the water and potatoes. Cook at a simmer for 30 minutes or so. Add the corn, and cook another 5 minutes. Add the shrimp and any other seafood you choose. Cook another 5 minutes, or until done: shrimp should be pink; clams and mussels fully open (discard any mussels or clams that do not open).

For traditional service, strain everything out of the broth and dump it in the middle of a newspaper-covered table for a savage free-for-all. While this method is great fun for a cookout, we usually end up straining everything into a large mixing bowl. In either case, serve it up with cocktail sauce, Dijon mustard, or whatever dips you like. Dig in! ◊

"Midwest Goes Southwest" Hotdish

Back when I first moved to Minnesota, I was a little horrified when some-one explained the concept of hotdish to me. It just sounded so . . . bland. If hotdish cooking was a requirement of my residency, I'd need to come up with something far more flavorful than cream of mushroom soup. Here is the result. **SERVES 6**

1 medium onion, thinly sliced

1 jalapeño, finely chopped

2 poblano chiles, thinly sliced

4 cloves garlic, chopped

2 tablespoons olive oil

1½ pounds skinless, boneless chicken breast, cut into bite-size pieces

3 ears fresh sweet corn, husks removed

2 (15-ounce) cans black beans, rinsed and drained

½ teaspoon red pepper flakes

1½ teaspoons cumin

2 (10.5-ounce) cans condensed cheese soup

½ cup salsa (preferably hot)

½ cup pitted, sliced black olives

2 cups shredded Monterey Jack cheese

2 pounds frozen potato "tots"

Preheat oven to 350 degrees. In a large pan over medium heat, cook onion, jalapeño, and poblanos, stirring often, until tender. Add garlic, olive oil, and chicken, and continue cooking until chicken is cooked all the way through, about 5 minutes.

Using a sharp knife, carefully cut kernels off the ears of corn. Add kernels to the pan along with black beans, red pepper flakes, and cumin. Stir well; cook for 2 minutes.

Pour mixture into a 9x13–inch baking dish. Stir in condensed soup, salsa, and black olives, mixing well to coat everything evenly. Sprinkle shredded cheese over mixture. Arrange potato "tots" in a single layer on top of the cheese. Bake for 50 minutes. Serve hot. ◇

SAVORY CORN CHEESECAKE

Who says cheesecake is only for dessert? This savory version is best served at least slightly warm. I like it best chilled first and then reheated to HOT in the microwave. Yum! SERVES 8–10

CRUST

1¼ cups finely chopped almonds (almond meal, almond flour)

½ cup grated Parmigiano-Reggiano cheese

⅓ cup butter, melted

pinch pepper

Mix together all ingredients until completely incorporated and moistened. Evenly distribute across the bottom of a 9-inch springform pan, pressing ingredients firmly and extending crust partway up the sides of the pan. Chill for at least 1 hour.

>>

CHEESECAKE

- 3 ears fresh sweet corn, husks removed
- ½ cup milk
- ½ small onion, diced
- 2 cloves garlic, pressed or minced
- 24 ounces cream cheese, softened
- 1 cup shredded provolone cheese
- ½ cup sour cream
- 6 large eggs
- 1 cup heavy cream
- 1 teaspoon salt
- ¼–½ teaspoon pepper

....

Preheat oven to 425 degrees. Using a sharp knife, carefully cut kernels off the ears of corn. Add kernels to a food processor or blender along with milk, onion, and garlic. Puree until very smooth, about 2 minutes. Transfer to a large mixing bowl.

Add to bowl of food processor cream cheese, provolone, sour cream, and eggs; pulse to combine. With motor running, carefully stream in heavy cream, and process just until well combined and smooth. Pour cheese mixture into corn mixture, and stir until well combined. Stir in salt and pepper.

Gently pour batter into prepared crust, and bake for 15 minutes. Reduce oven temperature to 325 degrees, and bake for an additional 50 minutes. Once baking time is complete—WITHOUT opening the oven—turn off the heat and allow cheesecake to cool in the oven for 2 hours.

Note: While this cheesecake is fantastic as is, it also works well when topped with any number of complementary items. Try roasted corn kernels, roasted red pepper, pesto, or crumbled bacon. ◊

Savory Corn Cheesecake

Hearty Corn and Black Bean Soup

When the weather starts to turn and the first few cold nights appear, this soup is a great way to welcome fall. Thick, warm, rich, and satisfying.
SERVES 6–8

2 large onions, chopped

1 pound bacon, chopped

2 pounds dried black beans

12½ cups chicken broth

1–2 bottles light-tasting beer, or use 2–4 cups water or additional chicken broth

6 ears fresh sweet corn, husks removed

juice and zest of 2 limes

6 ribs celery, chopped

3 green bell peppers, chopped

2 red bell peppers, chopped

1 yellow bell pepper, chopped

3 jalapeños, finely chopped

6 cloves garlic, pressed or minced

2 teaspoons cumin

1 teaspoon salt

1 teaspoon pepper

optional toppings: Cheddar cheese, sour cream, crumbled cooked bacon

In a large, heavy pot, cook onions and bacon over medium heat, stirring, until bacon is cooked but not crispy. Add black beans, chicken broth, and beer, and heat to boiling. Once mixture comes to a boil, stir it once, cover it with a lid, and remove from heat. Allow to sit for 1 hour. Return mixture to a boil. Reduce heat and simmer for 1 hour, stirring frequently.

Using a sharp knife, carefully cut kernels off the ears of corn. Add kernels to pot along with lime juice and zest, celery, peppers, jalapeño, garlic, and seasonings. Continue to simmer for another 20 minutes, until beans and all vegetables are tender and soup is quite thick. Serve hot, topped with Cheddar cheese, sour cream, and/or crumbled bacon. ◇

Roasted Corn Chowder

This base recipe for chowder can be customized in many ways. It requires a little bit of effort, but it's very much worth it. **SERVES 4**

6–7 ears fresh sweet corn, husks removed

3 tablespoons olive oil, divided

2 cups water, divided

2 ribs celery, chopped

1 small onion, chopped

4–5 red potatoes, cut into ½-inch chunks

1½ cups heavy cream, divided

salt and pepper

Roasted Corn Chowder

Prepare grill. Brush 3–4 corncobs with 2 tablespoons olive oil, and grill corn until as "done" as you like (I prefer some dark grill marks but not an overall char). Set aside to cool.

Using a sharp knife, carefully cut kernels off remaining ears of corn. Add kernels to a food processor or blender with 1 cup of the water. Puree until very smooth, about 2 minutes. In a medium pot over medium heat, cook celery and onion in remaining 1 tablespoon olive oil, stirring occasionally, until veggies are translucent and tender. Add corn puree, remaining cup of water, and potatoes. Bring to a boil, reduce heat, and simmer until potatoes are tender, about 25 minutes.

Carefully cut kernels off roasted cobs of corn. Add kernels to a food processor or blender and puree with ½ cup heavy cream until somewhat smooth, about 30 seconds. Add roasted corn puree and remaining heavy cream to the pot, and simmer until heated through. Season with salt and pepper to taste.

Variations

- Add some chopped roasted red peppers along with the roasted corn puree.
- Add some fresh basil and Parmesan cheese with the roasted corn puree.
- Add a couple of grilled jalapeños, finely chopped, with the roasted corn puree.
- Add about 2 cups shredded cheese along with the roasted corn puree.
- Top with crumbled bacon. ◇

COD AND CORN CHOWDER

Sometimes you want a chowder that comes together quickly and easily—and this one will not disappoint. The mushrooms, red pepper, corn, and cod not only taste really good together; they also produce a chowder that's actually fairly pretty—a departure from the soup's usual bland whiteness.

SERVES 8

....

½ pound bacon, sliced into small pieces

½ small onion, finely chopped

4–6 ounces button mushrooms, cleaned and chopped

1 red bell pepper, finely chopped

4 medium potatoes, cut into ½-inch cubes

3½ cups water

3 ears fresh sweet corn, husks removed

½ cup milk

1½ cups heavy cream

3–4 pounds cod loins, cubed

salt and pepper

....

In a medium saucepan, cook bacon over medium heat until cooked but not crispy. Add onion, mushrooms, and red pepper. Continue to cook, stirring occasionally, until onions are translucent and vegetables are softened. Add cubed potatoes and water. Increase heat to high, and cook at a rolling boil for 10 to 15 minutes or until potatoes are almost cooked through.

As the potatoes are cooking, use a sharp knife to carefully cut kernels off the ears of corn. Reserve half of the kernels, and add remaining kernels to a food processor or blender along with milk. Process until smooth.

When potatoes are about ready, add corn puree and heavy cream to pot and return mixture to a boil. Add cod and reserved corn kernels, and continue to cook for another 7 minutes or so, until cod is cooked through. Season with salt and pepper to taste. ◊

Cottage Pie

Cottage pie, made with ground beef and pork, is a variation on the traditional shepherd's pie dish, which uses lamb. This recipe makes a lot of food—two baking pans' worth. Freeze one for future meals and use the other for immediate eating. It makes the effort—and number of pots and pans used—even more worthwhile. **SERVES 12+**

- 4 pounds red potatoes, peeled or unpeeled, cut into 2-inch chunks
- 2 tablespoons olive oil
- 1 pound ground pork
- 1 pound lean ground beef
- 2 carrots, peeled and grated
- 2 parsnips, peeled and grated
- 1 medium onion, peeled and grated
- 2 cloves garlic, pressed or minced
- 1¾ cups chicken broth, divided
- 2 tablespoons cornstarch
- 2 teaspoons pepper, divided
- 2 teaspoons salt, divided
- 1 teaspoon dried rosemary
- ½ teaspoon dried savory, optional
- ½ cup chopped parsley
- 8 ears fresh sweet corn, husks removed
- 1 cup heavy cream
- 1 tablespoon granulated sugar
- 4 tablespoons (½ stick) butter
- 1½ cups sour cream

In a large pot of boiling water, cook potatoes until tender. While potatoes are cooking, combine oil, ground pork, ground beef, grated vegetables, and garlic in a large skillet. Cook over medium-high heat, stirring and breaking up meat chunks frequently, until meat is cooked through and veggies are tender, about 5 minutes. Whisk together 1½ cups chicken broth and cornstarch until smooth. Pour over meat mixture, and season with 1 teaspoon pepper, ½ teaspoon salt, rosemary, savory, and parsley. Continue to cook, stirring to combine, until broth mixture starts to thicken. Remove from heat.

Use a sharp knife to remove kernels from the corn. Place kernels in a medium pot along with heavy cream and sugar. Bring to a boil, reduce heat, and simmer for 10 minutes. Remove from heat, and season with salt to taste.

When potatoes are tender, drain and transfer to a large mixing bowl or the bowl of a stand mixer. Mash or whip for 30 seconds or so, until potatoes have broken down a bit. Add butter, remaining ¼ cup chicken broth, and sour cream, and continue to beat until smooth. Stir in remaining 1½ teaspoons salt and 1 teaspoon pepper.

Preheat broiler to high. Divide meat mixture evenly between two 9x13–inch pans. Divide corn mixture between the two pans, spreading evenly over the meat mixture. Spread potato mixture evenly over the corn, and broil until potatoes are as browned as you like them. Serve immediately, or cool to room temperature, cover with plastic wrap, and freeze for up to 2 months. Thaw before reheating portions in the microwave. ◊

GRILLED CORN QUESADILLAS

Quesadillas have been a favorite of mine since I was a kid. Best of all was one that utilized the fairly standard ingredients with the addition of corn. Nowadays, I prefer my quesadillas with many of those ingredients grilled beforehand, lending a wonderful, smoky taste to a traditional favorite.

SERVES 4

- 1 red bell pepper
- 1 poblano chile
- 1 medium onion, peeled
- 2 jalapeños
- 3 ears fresh sweet corn, husks removed
- ¼ cup olive oil
- ¼ cup chopped fresh cilantro
- ½–1 teaspoon cumin
- salt and pepper
- 8 flour tortillas
- 12 ounces (about 3 cups) shredded Monterey Jack cheese, divided
- salsa
- sour cream

Prepare grill. Preheat oven to 375 degrees. Slice red pepper and pob-lano chile into large flat pieces and onion into ½-inch-thick slices. Cut jalapeños in half, removing ribs and seeds if you prefer a milder que-sadilla. Brush vegetables and corncobs with olive oil. Grill everything until as "done" as you like (I prefer some dark grill marks but not an overall char). Remove items as they are ready; the pepper and chile will cook the fastest. Allow everything to cool.

Chop vegetables; place in a bowl. Use a sharp knife to remove kernels from the corn, and add to the bowl along with cilantro and cumin. Stir well, and season with salt and pepper to taste.

Arrange 4 tortillas on two baking sheets. Divide half of the cheese among the tortillas. Divide corn mixture among the tortillas, spread-ing evenly to within 1 inch of the edges. Top evenly with remaining cheese and finally with remaining tortillas. Bake for 15 minutes, until quesadillas are heated through and the cheese has melted. Cut into wedges and serve hot, with salsa and sour cream. ◊

Salsa Verde Tamales

The ingredient list may seem expensive, but this recipe makes a ton of tamales, as many as seventy. Very, very cheap meals. The tamales can be frozen: keep them in their wrappers and store them in freezer bags for up to three months. Allow the tamales to thaw, and then remove the husks before reheating in the microwave. Traditionally, tamales are served without sauce, but we prefer them with a bit of salsa. **MAKES APPROXIMATELY 30 TAMALES**

2 (8-ounce) packages dried corn husks

FILLING

6 large skinless, boneless chicken breasts, trimmed

1 cup beer

1 onion, finely chopped

6 jalapeños, finely chopped

2 tablespoons fresh lime juice

4 ears fresh sweet corn, husks removed

1–2 bunches fresh cilantro, chopped

2–3 (16-ounce) jars salsa verde

1 teaspoon salt

2 pounds (about 4 cups) colby-Jack cheese, shredded

MASA DOUGH

9 cups masa harina (finely ground corn flour)

5 tablespoons onion powder

3 teaspoons garlic salt

1½ tablespoons cumin

1½ tablespoons coriander

3 big handfuls parsley, chopped

3 tablespoons cayenne

7½ cups chicken broth

3 cups beer

3 cups lard or vegetable shortening

....

In a large bucket or stockpot, cover dried corn husks with hot water. When water has cooled, separate the husks, drain a bit of the water, and cover with more hot water. Let sit overnight.

In a large pot of boiling water, cook chicken breasts until cooked all the way through, about 10 to 12 minutes. Remove chicken breasts from water and allow to cool. Using two forks, shred the chicken into bite-size pieces. Place shredded chicken, beer, onion, jalapeños, and lime juice into a large pot and cook over medium heat, stirring frequently, until onion is translucent and jalapeño slices are soft. Most of the beer should have either cooked off or been absorbed by this point.

Use a sharp knife to remove kernels from the corn. Add kernels to the pot along with cilantro, salsa verde, and salt. Continue cooking until everything is thoroughly heated. Remove from heat, add shredded cheese, and stir until well combined. Set aside while you make the dough.

In a large bowl, mix together masa harina, onion powder, garlic salt, cumin, coriander, parsley, and cayenne, stirring until combined. In a large pot, combine chicken broth and beer, heating until about to boil. Remove from heat, and add the dry ingredient mixture. Stir until a smooth, thick dough forms. Allow to sit for 20 minutes. As dough is resting, whip lard with a stand or hand mixer until light and fluffy, 3 to 5 minutes. Add the lard to the dough, stirring until well combined and the consistency of peanut butter. If the dough is too thick, add a little more beer or chicken broth.

>>

Now, wrap the tamales. There are about ten million ways you can do this. Here's my technique. Pick out a large husk and a smaller husk. Overlap the wide ends slightly, with the small husk underneath the larger one. Measure about ⅓ cup masa dough onto the middle of the larger husk, spreading out slightly. Place a piece of plastic wrap on top of the dough and smooth dough into a longish rectangle. Remove plastic wrap and spread about ¼ cup filling in a long row up the middle of the dough rectangle, avoiding the last inch or so on each end.

Pick up the larger husk and fold the sides together, taking care to seal in the filling. Fold up the pointy end of the husk tightly against the bottom of the tamale. Fold in one long side of the husk snug against the tamale. Roll the tamale or fold in the other end. The basic idea is to completely envelop the sides and bottom, with no dough left exposed.

Place the rolled tamale seam-side down on the smaller husk. The remaining open side should be facing into the small husk, overlapping the husks by an inch or two. Roll the small husk around the tamale, and fold the pointy end of the small husk in over the seam, completely enveloping the main tamale roll.

Tie the tamale shut: the traditional method is to use long strips of (broken) soaked corn husks. Or use kitchen twine. Depending on how the wrap went, some tamales may require two ties. Repeat process about a million times.

Now steam the tamales. Depending on your equipment, you may need to do this in several batches. Put enough water in the bottom of the steamer to almost touch the bottom of the steam basket, and steam for about 2 hours, checking water level and adding more hot water as needed, until dough is cooked through and firmed up. Serve or freeze. ◇

Sweet Corn Risotto

Risotto is one of those dishes that many assume is difficult to make, but it truly is not. In fact, the repetition of the "add liquid, stir" steps can be downright relaxing. **SERVES 4–6**

....

3 ears fresh sweet corn, husks removed

6 cups chicken stock or broth, plus more as needed

⅔ cup white wine (not cooking wine)

1 tablespoon olive oil

1 medium onion, finely chopped

2 cloves garlic, pressed or minced

1½ cups arborio rice

1–2 tablespoons finely chopped fresh tarragon

2 tablespoons butter

1 cup grated Parmesan cheese

salt and pepper

....

Use a sharp knife to remove kernels from the corn. Reserve kernels in a bowl; add cobs to a large pot along with chicken stock or broth and white wine. Bring to a boil, reduce heat, and simmer for 10 minutes. Keep liquid at a simmer; discard cobs.

In a large saucepan, combine olive oil and onion. Cook over medium heat, stirring frequently, until onion is soft and translucent. Add garlic, rice, and about ½ cup of the chicken broth. Cook, stirring frequently, until almost all of the liquid is absorbed by the rice. One cup at a time, repeat this step until you have about 1 cup of liquid left.

Along with final amount of liquid, add fresh corn kernels and tarragon. Once rice is fully cooked and risotto is creamy and perfect, add butter and Parmesan cheese. Stir until everything is well combined and melty; season with salt and pepper to taste.

Variation: I love this dish with seafood on top—a bit of warm cooked crab, lobster, or scallops. Yum! ◊

CHICKEN AND CORN POTPIE

Comfort food at its finest. On a chilly fall day, what could be better than your own personal little dish of warm, gooey potpie topped with a flaky, crisp puff pastry cap? **SERVES 4**

....

 1 rotisserie chicken or 1 home-roasted chicken

 6 ears fresh sweet corn, husks removed

 5 cups chicken broth

12 tablespoons (1½ sticks) butter

 1 large onion, chopped

 4 ribs celery, chopped

¾ cup all-purpose flour

¼ cup heavy cream

⅓ cup finely chopped parsley

  salt and pepper

 2 frozen puff pastry sheets, thawed in the refrigerator

 1 large egg

....

Preheat oven to 350 degrees. Remove meat from chicken and cut into bite-size pieces. Set aside. Use a sharp knife to remove kernels from the corn. Reserve kernels with the chicken pieces, and add cobs to a medium pot along with chicken broth. Bring to a boil, reduce heat, and simmer for 10 minutes. Remove from heat; discard cobs.

In another large pot, melt butter over medium heat. Add onion and celery and cook—stirring frequently—until vegetables are tender and translucent. Reduce heat to low, add flour, and stir well to incorporate. Cook for 1 more minute, stirring constantly. Add heavy cream, stirring well until smooth and thickened. Add chicken, corn, and chicken broth, and bring just to a boil. Remove from heat, stir in the parsley, and season with salt and pepper to taste.

Divide the filling among 4 large (10-ounce) individual ramekins set on a cookie sheet. Cut each thawed puff pastry sheet in half, and lay one piece across the top of each filled ramekin. Press the edges along the ramekin rim if you like. Whisk egg with 2 tablespoons water, and use a pastry brush to coat the top of each potpie cap. Bake for about 25 minutes, until tops are puffy and golden brown.

Variations

- Add 6 strips crumbled crispy bacon into the filling just before transferring to ramekins.
- Puree half of the reserved corn kernels with a bit of the broth, then add puree back to the broth and stir well. ◇

Ham and Corn Skewers with Pineapple Bourbon Glaze

This recipe is based on my Easter ham recipe, which is far too tasty to relegate to a single season. The flavors that work so well with that ham—pineapple juice, mustard, and bourbon—also complement corn on the cob. It's a great marriage of flavors. **SERVES 4–6**

2–3 ears fresh sweet corn, husks removed

3 pounds fully cooked ham, trimmed and cut into 1-inch cubes

1 onion, sliced

2 green bell peppers, cut into 1-inch squares

1 (20-ounce) can pineapple chunks in juice, drained, ½ cup juice reserved

¼ cup bourbon

¼ cup honey

1 tablespoon Dijon mustard

2 cloves garlic, pressed or minced

salt and pepper

Use a sharp knife to cut corncobs into 1½-inch-thick rounds. Place cut corn in a large mixing bowl along with ham, onion, and green peppers.

In a smaller mixing bowl, whisk together all remaining ingredients, including the reserved pineapple chunks and juice, seasoning with salt and pepper to taste. Pour over skewer ingredients, tossing to coat. Cover with plastic wrap, and chill in the fridge for 1 hour or up to a day.

Heat the grill and thread corn, ham, onion, and green peppers onto metal skewers. Grill skewers until ingredients are nicely browned, brushing occasionally with remaining marinade. The time will vary depending on your grill. ◇

Corncob Jelly >

Condiments & Beverages

Corn Cob Jelly

*W*hether a condiment or a beverage, corn shines as a unique accent to a meal. Finish off a serving of grilled meat with corn relish, spread jewel-like corn jelly on a beautiful biscuit, or sip on fresh corn wine or soda. Delicious!

COMPOUND BUTTERS

Compound butter is an extremely simple thing: you take a soft stick of butter and mix stuff into it. Spices, fresh herbs, zest, finely chopped vegetables, whatever: if you can think of some sort of flavorful aromatic, odds are you can make a compound butter with it. This recipe is a springboard for your own ideas.

The casual nature of that description doesn't really do justice to compound butter's place in cuisine. It's a very basic part of fine French cooking. Compound butters were made ahead of time to add flavor to almost any dish. Melted compound butter would serve as a substitute for a sauce, while room temperature butters would be served alongside steak, vegetables, or seafood. Anchovy butter was quite popular, along with flavors such as truffle, tarragon, garlic, even wine.

Compound butters are a wonderful addition in any modern kitchen. Melt them over steak, use them as a sauce, drizzle them over popcorn, spread them on a sandwich. Since compound butters can be made either sweet or savory, the possibilities are endless. For the purposes of this cookbook, however, compound butters are amazing slathered on corn on the cob.

You can run wild on the flavors you choose because corn provides a flexible base. Basically, any fresh or dried herb or spice is fair game, as are items such as crumbled bacon, dried mushrooms, anchovies, mustard, pesto, crushed peppercorns, and so on.

Some other ideas:

- Dijon mustard.

- Caramelized onion.

- Finely chopped chipotles in adobo sauce, plus some of that sauce.

- Curry powder and a little chopped fresh cilantro add a bit of Asian flair; also include a small amount of finely chopped fresh mint and/or a pinch of cumin.

- For an Italian flavor, use grated Parmesan cheese, oregano, basil, and maybe a little garlic salt.

- Go southwest with some chili powder and cumin.

- Chopped jalapeños. Seriously.

Other savory flavors that work well with corn, alone or in combination: chervil, chives, cumin, lemon balm, lemon-garlic, lime and chili, onion, paprika, parsley, saffron, sage, thyme.

While savory flavors are most popular for corn on the cob, don't overlook the sweet possibilities. Adding a tablespoon or so of sugar or honey along with sweeter ingredients can yield spectacular flavor. Any kind of citrus zest works well. And, believe it or not, cinnamon is a popular choice in some areas.

....

How do you make it? Simple!

Take a stick or two of butter and allow it to come to room temperature, nice and soft. Stir in whatever flavoring agents you like, mixing and matching as desired. I recommend 2–3 tablespoons of solids (fresh herbs, zest) or around 1–1½ tablespoons of powders per stick of butter as a rough guide, but there's a lot of room to play. Vary the colors to make it pretty—for instance, combine mint and cilantro with curry powder.

>>

Whip butter and flavorings until everything is well distributed. Refrigerate for about 10 minutes, just long enough for the butter to firm up slightly but still be workable. Dump it out onto a section of plastic wrap and roll it into a log. (Alternatively, press it into an appropriately sized ramekin or other vessel.) Chill until firmly set.

Use the butter within a week. It can also be stored in the freezer for about a month.

....

Consider sharing the love: logs or little ceramic pots of compound butter make winning hostess gifts.

Logs: Peel the plastic wrap off the well-chilled log of compound butter. Wrap tightly with a clean piece of plastic wrap before rolling it up in a piece of something more decorative: parchment paper, cellophane, craft paper, etc. Tie off either end with some twine or ribbon, and label it with the flavor.

Pots: Press still-soft compound butter into a ceramic ramekin right after mixing it up. Use the back of a spoon to create a pretty swirl on top of the butter, then chill until firm. Place chilled ramekin in the middle of a large piece of cellophane, draw up all of the sides and corners, and secure on top with a bow. ◊

Compound Butters

CREAMY CORN DRESSING

If you're a fan of corn and a fan of creamy dressings, this recipe will brighten your salad plate. It combines the flavors of a traditional ranch dressing with fresh, sweet corn—delicious! **MAKES ABOUT 4 CUPS**

- 2 ears fresh sweet corn, husks removed
- 1 clove garlic, pressed or minced
- ½ cup buttermilk, plus up to ¼ cup more as needed
- ¾ cup mayonnaise
- ½ cup sour cream
- ¼ cup finely chopped fresh dill weed
- ¼ cup finely chopped parsley
- 2 teaspoons finely chopped fresh chives
- ½–1 teaspoon pepper
- ¼ teaspoon cayenne
- salt

Using a sharp knife, carefully cut kernels off the ears of corn. Add kernels to a food processor or blender along with garlic and ½ cup buttermilk. Process until corn is very smooth, about 2 minutes. Add mayonnaise and sour cream, and process until smooth and fully incorporated. Add dill, parsley, chives, pepper, and cayenne, and process for another 3 seconds. Season with salt to taste.

Chill for at least 30 minutes before serving to allow the flavors to meld. If dressing is thick, stir in additional buttermilk to reach desired consistency. ◊

QUICK CORN, TOMATO, AND BASIL CHUTNEY

This thick, non-pickled relish is a great way to add a ton of flavor to basic meat dishes. Try it over a pan-fried pork chop, alongside roasted chicken, or even with crab cakes. **MAKES ABOUT 4 CUPS**

- 2 ears fresh sweet corn, husks removed
- 2 cups cherry tomatoes, quartered
- ⅓ cup fresh basil leaves, sliced into ribbons
- 2 green onions, thinly sliced
- 2 tablespoons red wine vinegar
- 1 tablespoon olive oil
- salt and pepper

Using a sharp knife, carefully cut kernels off the ears of corn. Add kernels to a nonstick skillet along with quartered cherry tomatoes. Cook, stirring, over high heat for about 5 minutes. Remove from heat, stir in basil and green onions, and allow to cool to room temperature.

Whisk together red wine vinegar and olive oil until emulsified. Toss with cooled corn and tomato mixture, and season with salt and pepper to taste. Serve chilled or reheated.

Variation: If you want to get more elaborate—and enjoy a huge taste payoff—try grilling or roasting the tomatoes and corn before mixing ingredients together. ◊

CORN RELISH

I left a big jar of this corn relish at a friend's house as a welcome home gift. It didn't take long for her to message me a thank-you, saying, "It's DELICIOUS." When I let her know that we had plenty in case she ever wanted more, she replied: "I will take as much of this corn business as you're willing to give me. I want to pour it in a kiddie pool and lounge around in it." I think she liked it. For more details on proper canning methods, find a good preserving cookbook or go to www.freshpreserving.com. **MAKES ABOUT 5 QUARTS**

....

24 ears fresh sweet corn, husks removed

4 large green bell peppers, chopped

2 large onions, chopped

2–3 large tomatoes, chopped

4–5 ribs celery, chopped

2 jalapeños, chopped, ribs and seeds removed if desired

1½ cups granulated sugar

¼ cup salt

2 teaspoons turmeric

1 tablespoon celery seed

2 teaspoons dry mustard

5 cups white vinegar

....

Use a sharp knife to remove kernels from the cobs. Place kernels in a large pot. Add peppers, onions, tomatoes, celery, and jalapeños. In a medium bowl, mix together sugar, salt, turmeric, celery seed, and dry mustard. Add mixture to the pot, and stir well before adding the vinegar. Heat to a boil, then reduce heat and simmer for about 40 minutes.

Ladle into hot, sterilized canning jars (see pickling technique, pages 93–95). Affix sterilized lids and rims, and process in a hot water bath for 15 minutes. (Add 5 minutes for altitudes above 1,000 feet; add 10 minutes for altitudes over 6,000 feet.) Allow to cool overnight. Check all lids for a proper seal: they should have sucked down into a vacuum seal as the jars cooled. Store properly sealed jars for later use; refrigerate any that did not seal for use in the coming weeks. ◊

Corn Relish

CORNCOB JELLY

This jelly is a great way to use up the cobs left over from various "cut the kernels off the cob" recipes. The finished product actually tastes a lot like honey. **MAKES ABOUT 3 PINTS**

12 cobs sweet corn

8 cups water

1 tablespoon freshly squeezed lemon juice

1 (1.75-ounce) box powdered fruit pectin

4 cups granulated sugar

yellow food coloring, optional

If your cobs aren't "left over," cut the kernels off and save for another recipe. Add cobs and water to a large pot, and bring to a full rolling boil for 10 minutes. The liquid should be reduced by about half. Discard cobs; strain liquid through a couple layers of cheesecloth and measure. Add a little water, if needed, to bring the amount up to 3 cups. Return liquid to pot, add lemon juice and pectin, and bring to a boil. Add sugar, stirring well to dissolve. Bring pot to a full rolling boil for 1 complete minute, then remove from heat. Add a couple drops of food coloring, if desired.

Ladle into hot, sterilized canning jars (see pickling technique, pages 93–95, and page 90 for more canning information). Affix sterilized lids and rims, and process in a hot water bath for 15 minutes. (Add 5 minutes for altitudes above 1,000 feet; add 10 minutes for altitudes over 6,000 feet.) Allow to cool overnight. Check all lids for a proper seal: they should have sucked down into a vacuum seal as the jars cooled. Store properly sealed jars for later use; refrigerate any that did not seal for use in the coming weeks. ◊

PICKLED CORN ON THE COB

Did you know that you can pickle just about any kind of vegetable you can imagine? As I discovered on my "Great Pickling Binge of 2012," slices of whole corn on the cob pickle beautifully. I like to add several big slices of jalapeño to each jar—they're pretty AND they add a ton of flavor.

A few notes about pickling:

1. *The amount of brine you need will vary widely depend on the shape and size of your corncob slices, the size of the jar, and how well you pack the corn into the jar. Have a lot of extra vinegar on hand, and either make more brine than you think you'll need or be prepared to make more as you go. For a general idea of scale, this recipe made about 6 quart jars of pickles packed VERY tightly.*

2. *Pickling salt is usually available with the canning supplies in any grocery store. Do not use regular table salt: its anti-caking additives can make pickle brine go murky and ugly.*

3. *While you can employ previously used jars (when well washed and sterilized) for canning, you need new lids for each new batch. See page 90 for canning information. Safety first!* **MAKES 6–8 QUARTS**

....

12 ears fresh sweet corn, husks removed

BRINE

8 cups white vinegar

8 cups water

1 cup pickling salt

>>

PER PINT JAR (DOUBLE FOR QUART JARS):

½–1 teaspoon dill seed

1–2 cloves garlic, peeled and halved

¼ teaspoon whole black peppercorns

¼ teaspoon whole mustard seed

jalapeño slices, optional

CANNING EQUIPMENT

clean, sterilized canning jars and rings

new, never-used, sterilized canning lids

canning funnel

LARGE pot for processing

jar lifter (nice to have, not necessary if you can handle pain)

....

Use a very sharp, heavy knife to cut cobs of corn into 1½-inch-wide disks. Fill a large pot with at least 6 inches of water, and place over medium or high heat to bring it to a boil as you prepare the brine.

In another pot, combine vinegar, water, and salt. Bring to a boil, stirring well to dissolve the salt. As the brine heats up, measure the "per jar" ingredients into sterilized jars. Arrange sliced corncobs in the jars, packing them tightly: really try to cram as many pieces into each jar as you can.

Once brine comes to a boil, use a canning funnel to pour brine into prepared jars, leaving about ½ inch head space. Wipe off the top edges of the jar with a clean, wet towel, top each with a new, sterilized lid, and carefully screw on a clean lid ring. I like to use a kitchen towel for this: the jars are HOT! Carefully place jars of pickles into the boiling water pot, and process with water at a full boil for 25 minutes. Carefully remove them from the bath, and allow to cool overnight.

The next morning, check to make sure all of the jars achieved a proper seal. If when you push down in the middle of a lid it "pops," it did not seal. Any jars that didn't seal should be put in the fridge and used in the next few weeks.

Leave the properly sealed jars alone for at least a few days to allow the flavors to permeate the pickles. Store in a cool, dark place for up to 1 year; chill well before eating. Enjoy! ◇

Sweet Corn Liqueur

Corn liqueur may sound unusual, but it's actually a great way to preserve and enjoy the flavor of fresh sweet corn, picked at its peak. Serve chilled or at room temperature. **MAKES ABOUT 4 CUPS**

3 ears fresh sweet corn, husks removed

1 cup water

¾ cup granulated sugar

1½ cups vodka or bourbon

Using a sharp knife, carefully cut kernels off the ears of corn. Add kernels to a food processor or blender along with water. Process until corn is pureed. Transfer corn puree to a medium saucepan. Over medium heat, cook mixture until almost boiling, stirring frequently. Remove from heat, and allow to steep for 5 to 10 minutes. Strain corn mixture through a wire sieve into a clean bowl. Rinse pot and sieve with cool water. Line sieve with at least 3 layers of cheesecloth, and strain corn liquid through cheesecloth back into the pot. Add sugar, and stir until dissolved. Allow mixture to cool.

Once mixture is cool, add vodka or bourbon, starting with 1½ cups. Stir until well combined. Taste, and add more vodka or bourbon if you so desire. Transfer liqueur to a clean bottle or jar, cover, and store in the fridge for up to 3 weeks. ◇

Sweet Corn Crème Liqueur

Much like Sweet Corn Liqueur (page 95), this recipe provides another creative way to experience the sweet taste of corn in a whole other light—this time, with the added benefit of milk fat. Sweet, creamy, and so very delicious. **MAKES ABOUT 5 CUPS**

> 3 ears fresh sweet corn, husks removed
>
> 1 cup heavy cream
>
> 1 (14-ounce) can sweetened condensed milk
>
> 1½–2 cups vodka

Using a sharp knife, carefully cut kernels off the ears of corn. Add kernels to a food processor or blender along with heavy cream. Process until corn is pureed. Transfer corn puree to a medium saucepan. Over medium heat, cook mixture until almost boiling, stirring frequently. Remove from heat, and allow to steep for 5 to 10 minutes. Strain corn mixture through a wire sieve into a clean bowl. Rinse pot and sieve with cool water. Line sieve with at least 3 layers of cheesecloth, and strain corn liquid through cheesecloth back into the pot. Add sweetened condensed milk to corn liquid, and stir until well combined. Add vodka, starting with 1½ cups. Stir until well combined. Taste, and add more vodka if you so desire. Transfer liqueur to a clean bottle or jar, cover, and store in the fridge for up to 3 weeks. ◊

Quick Corn Soda

Corn soda is easy to make and very versatile. It cooks up in just minutes, and then you can make cream soda, run it through a soda machine, or just enjoy it as a quick soda mix, a little at a time. **MAKES ABOUT 3 CUPS SYRUP**

    3 ears fresh sweet corn, husks removed
1½ cups water
    2 cups granulated sugar
    carbonated or seltzer water

Using a sharp knife, carefully cut kernels off the ears of corn. Add kernels to a food processor or blender along with the water. Process until corn is pureed. Transfer corn puree to a medium saucepan. Over medium heat, cook mixture until almost boiling, stirring frequently. Reduce heat, and simmer for 5 more minutes. Remove from heat, and allow to steep for 10 minutes. Strain corn mixture through a wire sieve into a clean bowl. Rinse pot and sieve with cool water. Line sieve with at least 3 layers of cheesecloth, and strain corn liquid through cheesecloth back into the pot. Add sugar to corn liquid. Cook over medium heat, stirring until completely dissolved. Remove from heat, and cool to room temperature. Transfer syrup to a clean bottle or jar, cover, and store in the fridge for up to 3 weeks.

To use:

- Measure about 3 tablespoons soda syrup into a tall glass, top with carbonated or seltzer water, and stir gently to combine.
- Use in soda machines just as you would store-bought syrups.

For Corn Cream Soda: Add 1 tablespoon vanilla extract to cooled syrup before storing, stirring well to combine. ◊

Quick Corn Soda

Brewed Corn Soda

If you yearn for the taste of old-time sodas, this is a unique recipe for you. It requires a bit more commitment than the preceding recipe, but it produces the characteristic flavors of old-fashioned, brewed soda. **MAKES 2 LITERS**

....

    2 ears fresh sweet corn, husks removed
 ¾ cup water
    1 cup granulated sugar
    scant ¼ teaspoon bread yeast
    scant 2 liters distilled or bottled (not tap) water,
        at room temperature

....

Using a sharp knife, carefully cut kernels off the ears of corn. Add kernels to a food processor or blender along with ¾ cup water. Process until corn is pureed. Transfer corn puree to a medium saucepan. Over medium heat, cook mixture until almost boiling, stirring frequently. Reduce heat, and simmer 5 more minutes. Remove from heat, and allow to steep for 10 minutes. Strain corn mixture through a wire sieve into a clean bowl. Rinse pot and sieve with cool water. Line sieve with at least 3 layers of cheesecloth, and strain corn liquid through cheesecloth back into the pot. Add sugar to corn liquid. Cook over medium heat, stirring until completely dissolved. Remove from heat, and allow to cool for 5 minutes or so.

Use a funnel to transfer cooled soda syrup into a clean two-liter soda bottle. Add yeast and about 1 cup distilled water to the bottle, swirling to combine. Top with remaining water, leaving about 1 inch head space in the bottle. Cap tightly. Allow bottle to sit at room temperature for 1 to 3 days, just until the bottle gets hard (pressurized) from the carbonation that is building inside. Chill pressurized bottle upright in the fridge for a few days, allowing the yeast to settle at the bottom of the bottle.

>>

To serve, gently pour from the bottle, taking care not to disturb the settled yeast. When you get down to the last bit of soda in the bottle, discard it along with the yeast.

For Corn Cream Soda: Add ½–1 tablespoon vanilla extract to cooled syrup before adding yeast, stirring well to combine. ◊

CORNCOB WINE

Yes, you read that right: Corncob Wine. While this recipe has its roots in Prohibition-era underground brewing—and can be considered fairly trashy—it produces a uniquely flavored, sweet homemade wine. If you're like my husband and me—homebrewers who will wander a grocery store and think "Can we ferment that?"—this is a cool little recipe to try. The answer is "yes," by the way, and it's delicious. Visit my blog at www. celebrationgeneration.com for more information on beginning wine making. **MAKES 1 GALLON**

PER GALLON

- 6 ears fresh sweet corn, husks removed
- 1 gallon water, divided
- 9 cups granulated sugar
- 1 teaspoon yeast nutrient
- ½ teaspoon acid blend
- 1 packet wine yeast (Red Star Côte des Blancs)

2 (1-gallon) glass carboys and stoppers

1 airlock

siphon and tubing

wine bottles and caps

....

Using a sharp knife, carefully cut kernels off the ears of corn, reserving cobs. Working in batches, place kernels in a food processor or blender along with about ½ cup water. Process until corn is pureed, and transfer to a large pot along with the stripped cobs, remaining water, and sugar. Heat to almost boiling, stirring until sugar is dissolved. Simmer gently for 25 minutes, remove from heat, and stir in yeast nutrient and acid blend. Cover with sanitized pot lid, and cool to room temperature.

Use a sanitized funnel to transfer cooled mixture to a sanitized 1-gallon glass carboy. Sprinkle yeast into carboy, and cover with sanitized airlock. Let sit, undisturbed, overnight.

Within 48 hours, you should notice fermentation activity: bubbles in the airlock and carbonation or swirling in the liquid. This means you're good to go. Put the carboy somewhere cool (not cold), and leave it alone for a month or so. If it doesn't start fermenting, add fresh yeast: the original yeast may have been dead.

Using sanitized equipment, rack the clarified wine off the sediment into a clean, freshly sanitized 1-gallon carboy. Cap with sanitized airlock, and leave it alone for another 2 to 3 months.

When you've let it clarify as much as you have patience for—and no more sediment is being produced—move on to bottling. Using sanitized equipment, rack the wine into clean, sanitized wine bottles and cap them. Allow to age for a month or so before drinking. ◇

Atol de Elote

This hot corn beverage is popular in South America, with many regional variations. Atol *on its own refers to a hot corn drink;* elote *indicates one made with fresh corn rather than with hominy. While usually served as a beverage, depending on how starchy the corn is the result can be a hot, almost custardy pudding.* **SERVES 4**

6 ears fresh sweet corn, husks removed

4 cups milk, divided

½–1 cup granulated sugar

1–2 (3-inch-long) cinnamon sticks

¼–½ teaspoon salt

ground cinnamon, optional

Using a sharp knife, carefully cut kernels off the ears of corn. Add kernels to a food processor or blender along with about half the milk. Process until corn is very smooth, about 2 minutes. Transfer corn puree to a medium pot along with the remaining milk. Bring to a boil, stirring frequently. Remove from heat. Strain corn mixture through a wire sieve into a clean bowl. Rinse pot and sieve with cool water. Line sieve with at least 3 layers of cheesecloth, and strain corn liquid through cheesecloth back into the pot. Add sugar, cinnamon stick(s), and salt to corn liquid, stirring until well combined. Return to a near boil, reduce heat, and allow to simmer for 5 minutes, stirring frequently. Distribute hot atole into serving mugs, and garnish with a pinch of ground cinnamon if desired. ◊

"Corn Syrup"

Yes, the quotation marks are intentional. This concoction isn't corn syrup in the traditional sense—you wouldn't want to use it in candy making, for instance. No, it's a mildly corn-flavored, thick simple syrup that is great poured on sweet corn pancakes, drizzled over ice cream, and used in cocktails. **MAKES ABOUT 5 CUPS**

- 5 cobs sweet corn, kernels removed, cut into 1-inch chunks
- 6 cups water
- 6 cups granulated sugar
- 1 teaspoon salt

Place corncob chunks in a large pot. Cover with the water, bring to a boil, reduce heat, and simmer for about 30 minutes. Liquid should be reduced to about half of the starting volume.

Remove corncob pieces from the water; discard. Strain corn liquid through a wire sieve into a clean bowl. Rinse pot and sieve with cool water. Line sieve with at least 3 layers of cheesecloth, and strain corn liquid through cheesecloth back into the pot. Add sugar and salt, stirring well.

Return mixture to a boil, reduce heat, and simmer for another 10 minutes. Remove from heat, and cool to room temperature. Transfer syrup to a bottle or jar, and cover with a tight-fitting lid. Store in the fridge for up to 3 months.

As the syrup ages, it may begin to recrystallize. If this happens, heat it and add a tablespoon of water, stirring until it returns to a smooth, syrupy consistency. ◇

Desserts

W hile corn is technically a grain—and usually treated as a vegetable—the sweet taste of fresh summer corn can be used in desserts with spectacular results. This chapter focuses on the sweet side of corn. Try fresh sweet corn in panna cottas, as ice cream, in custards, in mousse, or done up as fancy truffles. So many possibilities!

SWEET CORN PANNA COTTA

Steeping dairy ingredients with fresh sweet corn provides the base of a wide variety of creamy desserts—the ideal way to show off the grain's subtle, sweet flavor. One of the most simple to make is panna cotta. This recipe produces a beautiful, pale dessert, with the clear flavor of corn shining through. **MAKES ABOUT 4 SERVINGS**

....

  1½ teaspoons unflavored gelatin powder

   3 tablespoons cold water

2–3 ears fresh sweet corn, husks removed

  ¾ cup milk

   1 cup heavy cream

  ½ cup granulated sugar

  ½ cup sour cream

    toppings: Glazed Nuts, Candied Bacon, Blueberry Sauce, or Salted Caramel Sauce (pages 126–29)

....

Sprinkle the gelatin over the cold water in a small bowl and let soak for 5 minutes.

>>

Using a sharp knife, carefully cut kernels off the ears of corn. Add kernels to a food processor or blender along with the milk. Process until corn is rendered into small pieces. Pour into a saucepan along with heavy cream. Heat corn and liquid mixture just to a simmer, stirring occasionally; do not let it boil. Remove from heat, and allow to steep for 10 minutes.

Once mixture has steeped, pour it through a fine-mesh strainer into a clean saucepan; discard kernel pulp. Add sugar, and heat mixture over medium just to a simmer once again, stirring to dissolve sugar. Meanwhile, microwave the gelatin on high for about 15 seconds or until melted.

Once the milk mixture has come to a simmer, remove it from the heat. Whisk in the gelatin until fully incorporated and the mixture is smooth. Add sour cream, whisking until fully incorporated and smooth. Pour into 4 greased ramekins or custard cups. Chill for at least 2 hours, until set.

Top with Glazed Nuts, Candied Bacon, Blueberry Sauce, or Salted Caramel Sauce. ◊

SWEET CORN CRÈME BRÛLÉE

A unique variation on a very traditional dessert. The crunch of the sugar crust is the perfect foil for the creamy goodness of the corn-flavored custard.

MAKES 6 SMALL SERVINGS

8 large egg yolks

¾ cup granulated sugar, divided

2 cups heavy cream, divided

2–3 ears fresh sweet corn, husks removed

Preheat oven to 325 degrees. Combine egg yolks and ¼ cup sugar in a bowl, whisking until the mixture becomes thick and pale yellow. Add approximately half of the heavy cream, whisking until incorporated and smooth.

Using a sharp knife, carefully cut kernels off the ears of corn, placing them in a large saucepan. Once ears are completely stripped of kernels, chop cobs into 2- to 3-inch lengths and add them to the pot along with ¼ cup sugar and remaining heavy cream.

Heat corn and liquid mixture just to a simmer, stirring occasionally; do not let it boil. Remove from heat, and allow to steep for 30 minutes. Once mixture has steeped, pour it through a fine-mesh strainer into a clean saucepan; discard kernels and cob pieces. Heat mixture over medium just to a simmer once again.

Remove from heat. Slowly drizzle hot cream mixture into the egg mixture, whisking constantly. Pour into 6 ramekins or custard cups, and arrange in a large pan. Carefully add water to the large pan, filling to about halfway up the sides of the ramekins.

Bake until custard is set but wiggles in the middle—about 45 to 50 minutes. Remove from oven, allow to cool to room temperature, and then chill for at least 2 hours. When ready to serve, sprinkle 2–3 teaspoons sugar evenly over each custard. Use a small, handheld kitchen torch to melt sugar, or place custards under the broiler for a few minutes. ◊

SWEET CORN MOUSSE

When it comes to mousse, there are two main styles—"traditional" and "easy." Traditional mousse is made with raw egg yolks and/or egg whites. While this preparation is perfectly safe for the vast majority of the population, pregnant women, the elderly, and immune compromised individuals may want to opt for the easy version, which does not contain any raw eggs.

EASY SWEET CORN MOUSSE
serves 6–8

2–3 ears fresh sweet corn, husks removed
2 cups heavy cream
⅓ cup granulated sugar
1½ teaspoons unflavored gelatin powder
⅓ cup cold water

Using a sharp knife, carefully cut kernels off the ears of corn, placing them in a large saucepan. Once ears are completely stripped of kernels, chop cobs into 2- to 3-inch lengths and add them to the pot along with heavy cream and sugar.

Heat corn and liquid mixture just to a simmer, stirring occasionally; do not let it boil. Remove from heat, and allow to steep for 30 minutes. Once mixture has steeped, pour it through a fine-mesh strainer and into a clean mixing bowl; discard kernels and cob pieces. Cover bowl with plastic wrap, and chill well—at least 1 hour.

In a small bowl, sprinkle gelatin over water and let soak for 5 minutes. Microwave mixture on high in 10-second increments until gelatin dissolves into the water.

Remove corn liquid from the fridge. Whip until stiff peaks form, then carefully fold in the gelatin mixture, stirring until combined. Pour into 6 to 8 serving glasses, and chill until set, about 2 hours.

TRADITIONAL SWEET CORN MOUSSE

serves 4–6

2–3 ears fresh sweet corn, husks removed

1 cup heavy cream

¼ cup granulated sugar

2 large egg yolks

3 large egg whites

....

Using a sharp knife, carefully cut kernels off the ears of corn, placing them in a large saucepan. Once ears are completely stripped of kernels, chop cobs into 2- to 3-inch lengths and add them to the pot along with heavy cream.

Heat corn and liquid mixture just to a simmer, stirring occasionally; do not let it boil. Remove from heat, and allow to steep for 30 minutes. Once mixture has steeped, run it through a fine-mesh strainer into a clean mixing bowl; discard kernels and cob pieces. Cover bowl with plastic wrap, and chill well—at least 1 hour.

Combine sugar and egg yolks, beating until pale yellow and fluffy. Stir in heavy cream mixture a little at a time, until fully incorporated. Whip until stiff peaks form, then transfer bowl to fridge.

In a separate bowl, whip the egg whites until stiff peaks form. Carefully fold in chilled whipped cream mixture, stirring until combined. Pour into 4 to 6 serving glasses, and chill until set, about 2 hours. ◊

SWEET CORN FLAN

Much like with the crème brûlée (page 106), flan is a great way to incorporate sweet corn flavor into an elegant dessert. And, given the origins of the grain, it's especially fitting to make a corn-flavored version of this popular Latin American dish. **SERVES ABOUT 8**

2–3 ears fresh sweet corn, husks removed

2 cups heavy cream

2½ cups granulated sugar, divided

¼ cup water

8 large eggs

2 cups milk

Preheat oven to 375 degrees. Using a sharp knife, carefully cut kernels off the ears of corn, placing them in a large saucepan. Once ears are completely stripped of kernels, chop cobs into 2- to 3-inch lengths and add them to the pot along with heavy cream. Heat corn and liquid mixture just to a simmer, stirring occasionally; do not let it boil. Remove from heat, and allow to steep for 30 minutes.

Combine 2 cups of the sugar with water in a small saucepan over medium heat. Stir until sugar is a light golden brown, about 15–20 minutes. Pour this caramel mixture into a generously greased flan pan, quiche dish, or glass baking dish.

Once corn mixture has steeped, pour it through a fine-mesh strainer into a clean mixing bowl; discard kernels and cob pieces. Combine eggs and ½ cup sugar, and beat until well blended, pale, and smooth. Alternate adding cream mixture and milk to eggs a little at a time, stirring until fully incorporated. Slowly and carefully pour over the caramel in the prepared pan.

Set flan pan inside a larger baking pan. Carefully add water to the large pan, filling to about halfway up the sides of the flan pan. Bake for 45 to 60 minutes or until custard is set. Cool to room temperature, then chill completely.

To serve, run a knife around the outside edge of the flan to loosen. Place a serving plate face-down over the baking dish, and carefully invert. ◇

Sweet Corn Ice Cream

This recipe is more properly for a frozen custard, but the line between custard and ice cream has blurred somewhat in modern usage. Nonetheless, this dessert is becoming popular at summer festivals and other events—a far cry from the bizarre reactions I received when I created this recipe back in 2006. **MAKES ABOUT 1½ QUARTS**

- 3 ears fresh sweet corn, husks removed
- 2 cups whole milk
- 8 large egg yolks
- ¾ cup granulated sugar
- ¼ teaspoon salt
- 2 cups heavy cream

Using a sharp knife, carefully cut kernels off the ears of corn, placing them in a large saucepan. Once ears are completely stripped of kernels, chop cobs into 2- to 3-inch lengths and add them to the pot along with milk. Heat corn and milk mixture just to a simmer, stirring occasionally; do not let it boil. Remove from heat, and allow to steep for 30 minutes. Once corn mixture has steeped, remove and discard cob pieces.

Combine egg yolks, sugar, and salt in a medium mixing bowl. Whisk for a few minutes, until fluffy, pale yellow, and smooth. Add heavy cream, whisking until well incorporated.

Pour egg mixture into corn mixture, whisking to incorporate. Cook over medium heat, stirring constantly, until mixture thickens—it should be thick enough to coat the back of a spoon. Remove from heat, cool to room temperature, and then chill thoroughly until ready to use.

Follow your ice cream maker's instructions to freeze custard mixture. Serve immediately for a soft ice cream, or freeze for at least 2 hours for a firmer ice cream. ◊

CREAMY CORN CHEESECAKE

Corn makes a fantastic cheesecake, whether savory (see page 61) or sweet.

SERVES 10–12

....

3 ears fresh sweet corn, husks removed

1 cup heavy cream

32 ounces cream cheese, at room temperature

1½ cups granulated sugar

1 cup sour cream

6 large eggs

juice of 1 lemon (about 3 tablespoons)

1 cheesecake crust (recipe follows)

optional toppings: Glazed Nuts, Candied Bacon,
  Blueberry Sauce, or Salted Caramel Sauce (pages 126–29)

....

Preheat oven to 425 degrees. Using a sharp knife, carefully cut kernels off the ears of corn, placing them in a large saucepan. Once ears are completely stripped of kernels, chop cobs into 2- to 3-inch lengths and add them to the pot along with heavy cream. Heat corn and liquid mixture just to a simmer, stirring occasionally; do not let it boil. Remove from heat, and allow to steep for 30 minutes.

In stand mixer, beat together cream cheese and sugar until smooth. Add sour cream, eggs, and lemon juice. Beat on low to medium-low speed until smooth.

Once corn mixture has steeped, pour it through a fine-mesh strainer into the stand mixer bowl; discard kernels and cob pieces. Beat cheesecake batter on low to medium-low speed until smooth. Gently pour batter into prepared crust. Chill for 10 minutes.

>>

Bake for 15 minutes, then reduce oven temperature to 325 degrees and bake for another 50 minutes. Once baking time is complete, turn off the oven and allow cake to cool—WITHOUT opening the oven door— for 2 hours. Chill cake thoroughly before serving.

Serve plain, or top with Glazed Nuts, Candied Bacon, Blueberry Sauce, or Salted Caramel Sauce.

BASIC CHEESECAKE CRUST

Use graham cracker crumbs for a basic, traditional cheesecake crust. Chocolate sandwich cookies, vanilla cookies, or any other type of dry cookie can be used to customize crust flavor. Or substitute finely chopped nuts for all or part of the crumbs.

....

1½ cups crumbs (see head note)

¼ cup granulated sugar

5 tablespoons butter, melted

....

Stir together all ingredients until completely incorporated and moistened. Evenly distribute across the bottom of a 9-inch springform pan. Press ingredients firmly, extending crust partway up the sides of the pan. Chill for at least 1 hour before using. ◊

Sweet Corn Pastry Cream

Pastry cream—also known as crème pâtissière—is a very thick, rich custard. It's used in many French pastries—such as éclairs and cream puffs—and also as filling for tarts and cakes. This recipe is easily doubled or tripled.

MAKES ABOUT 1 CUP

3 ears fresh sweet corn, husks removed

1 cup milk

3 large egg yolks

¼ cup granulated sugar

2 tablespoons all-purpose flour

2 tablespoons butter

Using a sharp knife, carefully cut kernels off the ears of corn, placing them in a large saucepan. Once ears are completely stripped, chop cobs into 2- to 3-inch lengths and add them to the pot along with milk.

Heat corn and liquid mixture just to a simmer, stirring occasionally; do not let it boil. Remove from heat, and allow to steep for 20 minutes. Once mixture has steeped, pour it through a fine-mesh strainer into a mixing bowl; discard kernels and cob pieces.

In a separate bowl, whisk yolks together with sugar until fluffy and pale yellow. Add flour, whisking until incorporated and smooth. Set aside.

In a small saucepan, bring corn milk to a light boil. Measure about ¼ cup of the hot milk liquid, and stream slowly into egg mixture, whisking until it is completely incorporated and mixture is smooth. Repeat with another ¼ cup of hot liquid. Remove saucepan from heat, and pour egg mixture into milk mixture, whisking constantly. Once fully incorporated and smooth, return to low heat. Continue whisking, cooking until mixture is very thick. Remove from heat, and whisk in butter until fully incorporated and smooth. Cover with plastic wrap, and chill until needed. ◊

CREAM PUFFS

Cream puffs are a great way to showcase your Sweet Corn Pastry Cream (page 115)—and they are quite easy to make.

Cream puffs start out with pâte à choux, or choux pastry, a basic recipe that's used to make everything from cream puffs and éclairs to gougères and churros. It doesn't contain any leavening ingredients (yeast, baking powder, baking soda, etc.), instead relying on its high moisture content to puff during baking. When the pastry is baked at a high temperature, the water in the mixture becomes steam and creates large air pockets in the final product. SERVES 4–6

PÂTE À CHOUX

- 1 cup water
- 8 tablespoons (1 stick) butter
- 1 teaspoon granulated sugar
- ½ teaspoon salt
- 1 cup all-purpose flour
- 3 large eggs
- 2 large egg whites

Preheat oven to 425 degrees. Line a baking sheet with parchment paper or use a nonstick baking sheet. Do not grease the pan—doing so will cause the pastries to flatten.

Add water, butter, sugar, and salt to a medium saucepan, and heat to a boil, stirring to combine. Remove from heat, and add flour all at once, stirring until well incorporated.

Reduce heat to medium, and return saucepan to stovetop. Cook for another minute or so, stirring until the dough comes together and leaves the sides of the pan. Transfer dough to the bowl of a standing mixer. Using the paddle attachment, beat the dough for a minute or so to allow it to cool slightly.

Meanwhile, beat together eggs and egg whites in a small bowl. With the mixer set to medium, add egg mixture to dough a little at a time, allowing eggs to fully incorporate into the dough before adding more. (It may look like a separating mess, but I promise it will come together!)

When all of the eggs are incorporated and the dough is smooth and shiny, it's ready to pipe. It'll be soft and a bit sticky but more or less able to hold its shape. Pipe it out according to your desired use (below), and bake for the time indicated.

Cream Puffs

Using a pastry bag with a medium/large round or star tip, pipe out rounds that are about 2 to 2½ inches in diameter and 1½ inches tall, leaving 2 to 3 inches between mounds. Use a moistened finger to pat down any peaks of dough that form as you finish piping.

Bake for 12 minutes, then—WITHOUT opening the oven door—reduce oven temperature to 350 degrees and bake for another 35 minutes. Crack the oven door open a few inches, turn off the heat, and allow the puffs to cool in the oven for 30 minutes. This step allows the insides to dry out, providing a stronger structure to prevent collapse.

Once puffs are completely cool, cut in half horizontally, and fill with Sweet Corn Pastry Cream (page 115), dust with powdered sugar, drizzle with White Chocolate Corn Glaze (page 120), and/or serve with fresh fruit or berries.

>>

Profiteroles

Using spoons or a pastry bag, make tablespoon-size mounds of batter, leaving 2 inches of space between each. Use a moistened finger to pat down any peaks of dough that form as you finish piping.

Bake for 12 minutes, then—WITHOUT opening the oven door—reduce oven temperature to 350 degrees and bake for another 25 minutes. Crack the oven door open a few inches, turn off the heat, and allow the puffs to cool in the oven for 30 minutes. This step allows the insides to dry out, providing a stronger structure to prevent collapse.

Fill a pastry bag with your choice of Sweet Corn Pastry Cream (page 115), Pudding (page 121), or Mousse (page 108). Once puffs are completely cool, jam the tip of the pastry bag into the side of a puff, and fill. Dust with powdered sugar, or drizzle with White Chocolate Corn Glaze (page 120).

Éclairs

Using a pastry bag with a large round or star tip, pipe out logs that are about 2 inches by 5 to 6 inches, leaving 2 inches between logs. Use a moistened finger to pat down any peaks of dough that form as you finish piping.

Bake for 12 minutes, then—WITHOUT opening the oven door—reduce oven temperature to 350 degrees and bake for another 30 minutes. Crack the oven door open a few inches, turn off the heat, and allow the puffs to cool in the oven for 30 minutes. This step allows the insides to dry out, providing a stronger structure to prevent collapse.

Once logs are completely cool, cut in half horizontally, and fill with your choice of Sweet Corn Pastry Cream (page 115), Pudding (page 121), or Mousse (page 108). Dip the tops in White Chocolate Corn Glaze (page 120), and chill before serving.

Mini Éclairs

Using a pastry bag with a medium/large round or star tip, pipe out logs that are about 1 inch by 2 inches, leaving 2 inches between logs. Use a moistened finger to pat down any peaks of dough that form as you finish piping.

Bake for 12 minutes, then—WITHOUT opening the oven door—reduce oven temperature to 350 degrees and bake for another 20 minutes. Crack the oven door open a few inches, turn off the heat, and allow the puffs to cool in the oven for 30 minutes. This step allows the insides to dry out, providing a stronger structure to prevent collapse.

Fill a pastry bag with your choice of Sweet Corn Pastry Cream (page 115), Pudding (page 121), or Mousse (page 108). Once puffs are completely cool, jam the tip of the pastry bag into the side of a puff, and fill. Dip the tops in White Chocolate Corn Glaze (page 120), and chill before serving. ◊

WHITE CHOCOLATE CORN GLAZE

MAKES ABOUT 1 CUP

....

- 1 ear fresh sweet corn, husk removed
- ½ cup heavy cream
- 6 ounces white chocolate, finely chopped

....

Using a sharp knife, carefully cut kernels off the ear of corn, placing them in a medium saucepan. Once corn is completely stripped of kernels, chop cob into 2- to 3-inch lengths and add them to the pot along with heavy cream.

Heat corn and liquid mixture just to a simmer, stirring occasionally; do not let it boil. Remove from heat, and allow to steep for 20 minutes. Place white chocolate in a glass or metal mixing bowl, and set aside.

Once corn mixture has steeped, pour it through a fine-mesh strainer twice, ending with the mixture back in the pot: discard kernels and cob pieces.

Heat corn cream to a boil, then remove from heat. Pour hot cream over white chocolate, and let sit for 3 to 5 minutes. Starting in the middle of the bowl, slowly begin stirring the chocolate and cream until all of the chocolate is melted and the cream has disappeared into it: it should be smooth.

Glaze can be made a day or two in advance and stored, covered, in the fridge. Warm in the microwave for 20 to 30 seconds when ready to use. ◊

SWEET CORN PUDDING

Such a simple dessert, pudding is a great way to showcase the familiar flavor of sweet corn. Serve this chilled or, better yet, warm. **SERVES 6**

- 3 ears fresh sweet corn, husks removed
- 3 cups whole milk, divided
- ½ cup granulated sugar
- ¼ cup cornstarch
- ⅛ teaspoon salt
- 2 tablespoons butter

Using a sharp knife, carefully cut kernels off the ears of corn, placing them in a medium saucepan. Once corn is completely stripped of kernels, chop cobs into 2- to 3-inch lengths and add them to the pot along with 2 cups of the milk.

Heat corn and liquid mixture just to a simmer, stirring occasionally; do not let it boil. Remove from heat, and allow to steep for 20 minutes. Once corn mixture has steeped, pour it through a fine-mesh strainer twice, ending with the mixture back in the pot; discard kernels and cob pieces. Add sugar to the corn milk, and heat just to a simmer, stirring occasionally.

Meanwhile, whisk together remaining 1 cup milk, cornstarch, and salt until smooth. Pour into the hot milk, whisking constantly. Whisk over medium heat until mixture is thick and coats the back of a spoon, being careful to not allow it to boil. Remove from heat, stir in butter, and pour into serving dishes. Chill completely before serving.

Variations

- Melt 8 ounces white chocolate, and stir into pudding along with the butter.
- Substitute coconut cream for half of the milk. ◊

White Chocolate Sweet Corn Truffles

The prices for commercially produced truffles suggest they are much more labor intensive and specialized than is actually the case. Here is a quick and easy recipe for sweet corn truffles—unique, delicious, and elegant.

MAKES 20–30 TRUFFLES

....

- 3 ears fresh sweet corn, husks removed
- ½ cup heavy cream
- 12 ounces good-quality white chocolate chips
- 2 tablespoons butter
- powdered sugar

....

Using a sharp knife, carefully cut kernels off the ears of corn, placing them in a medium saucepan. Once ears are completely stripped of kernels, chop cobs into 2- to 3-inch lengths and add them to the pot along with heavy cream.

Heat corn and liquid mixture just to a simmer, stirring occasionally; do not let it boil. Remove from heat, and allow to steep for 20 minutes. Place white chocolate chips in a glass or metal mixing bowl, and set aside.

Once corn mixture has steeped, pour it through a fine-mesh strainer twice, ending with the mixture back in the pot; discard kernels and cob pieces. Add butter to the pot. Heat corn cream to a boil; remove from heat. Pour hot cream mixture into the bowl of white chocolate. Let sit for 3 to 5 minutes. Starting in the middle of the bowl, slowly begin stirring the chocolate and cream until all of the chocolate is melted and the cream has disappeared into it: it should be smooth.

Cover with plastic wrap, preferably resting right on top of the surface to prevent a skin from forming while it cools. Chill in the fridge for at least an hour or two, until the ganache mixture is pretty solid. Once solid, scoop out small amounts (a teaspoon or two), and roll them into balls. Try to handle the ganache as quickly as possible, or it will melt.

Once all of the ganache is rolled into balls, wash and dry hands, then roll ganache centers in powdered sugar. Store in an airtight container for up to 1 week. ◊

Easy White Chocolate Sweet Corn Fudge

Not the most elegant dish, but a quick and easy way to get your sweet corn fix—in dessert form. **MAKES AN 8x8-INCH PAN**

2 ears fresh sweet corn, husks removed

1 (14-ounce) can sweetened condensed milk

3 cups white chocolate chips

pinch salt

Line an 8-inch-square pan with parchment paper or grease pan generously with butter. Using a sharp knife, carefully cut kernels off the ears of corn. Add kernels to a food processor or blender along with sweetened condensed milk. Puree for 30 seconds.

Combine white chocolate chips and corn puree in a saucepan. Cook over medium-low heat, stirring frequently, until chocolate melts and mixture is smooth. (Alternatively, combine ingredients in a microwave-safe bowl and heat on high for 30-second intervals, stirring between each, until chocolate is melted and mixture is smooth.) Remove from heat, and stir in salt. Spread into prepared pan; chill until set. ◊

White Chocolate Sweet Corn Truffles

CREAMY SWEET CORN POPSICLES

The texture of these popsicles is perfect—smooth and creamy and satisfying. The pale yellow frozen pops are a great way to enjoy late-summer's corn bounty anytime. Depending on how sweet your corn is, you may want to use less sugar (¼ cup) for very sweet corn or more (½ cup) for corn that may be past its peak. Adjust for personal taste. **MAKES 4 OR MORE POP-SICLES, DEPENDING ON SIZE OF MOLD**

....

4 ears fresh sweet corn, husks removed

2 cups milk, divided

¼–½ cup granulated sugar (see head note)

salt

....

Using a sharp knife, carefully cut kernels off the ears of corn. Add kernels to a food processor or blender along with about 1 cup of the milk. Process until corn is very smooth, about 2 minutes. Transfer corn puree to a medium pot and add remaining milk. Bring to a boil, stirring frequently. Remove from heat.

Strain corn mixture through a wire sieve into a clean bowl. Rinse pot and sieve with cool water. Line sieve with at least 3 layers of cheesecloth; strain corn liquid through cheesecloth back into the pot; discard solids. Add sugar and a pinch of salt, and stir until fully dissolved. Allow to cool to room temperature.

Divide mixture into ice pop molds, small paper cups, or even ice cube trays. Place a popsicle stick into each cavity, and freeze overnight. ◊

Glazed Nuts

While these nuts are tasty on their own as a dessert, they're also a perfect topping for many of the corn desserts featured in this chapter. I like cashews, walnuts, or pecans for use on corn recipes, but feel free to experiment. You can choose almonds, peanuts—pretty much any nut you prefer. Use just one type or a mix of your favorites. **MAKES 1 POUND**

1 pound shelled nuts (see head note)

1 cup granulated sugar

2 tablespoons butter, melted

Line 2 cookie sheets with parchment paper. Combine nuts, sugar, and melted butter in a large, heavy pan. Cook over medium heat, stirring frequently, until sugar melts, turns golden, and coats the nuts—this will take 5 to 10 minutes.

Divide nuts between the cookie sheets, spreading loosely across each. Allow the nuts to cool completely; store in an airtight container. ◇

Candied Bacon Dessert Topping

Not so much a recipe, but more of a how-to. Use as much bacon as you think you'll need, and enough brown sugar to coat it.

....

bacon (ideally thick cut)

brown sugar

....

Preheat oven to 350 degrees; line a baking sheet with parchment paper. In a large mixing bowl, coat bacon slices with brown sugar. Arrange bacon in a single layer on baking sheet; sprinkle with additional brown sugar. Bake for 25 to 30 minutes, or until desired level of crispness. Allow to cool slightly, then crumble. ◊

Salted Caramel Sauce

Salted caramel is a recently popular flavor, used for almost any kind of dessert imaginable. The rich flavor of caramel with a bite of saltiness works really well as a foil to the creamy, corny desserts in this chapter. This sauce will keep in the fridge for as long as two to three weeks: just warm and stir before serving over your choice of dessert.

Be absolutely sure that the butter and cream are at room temperature or even a bit warmer: adding cold ingredients to the caramel can cause it to seize and turn into a crystallized mess. **MAKES ABOUT 3 CUPS**

....

2 cups granulated sugar

¼ cup corn syrup

1½ cups (3 sticks) butter, at room temperature (see head note)

1 cup heavy cream, at room temperature (see head note)

1 tablespoon sea salt

....

>>

In a large pot combine sugar and corn syrup. Bring to a boil over medium-high heat, gently stirring the mixture just until the sugar dissolves, trying not to splash much of it up the sides of the pot. Once the sugar has dissolved, reduce heat to medium and stop stirring— just swirl the pan gently every once in a while as it cooks.

Use a candy thermometer to keep an eye on the temperature of the caramel as it begins to turn golden brown. Once it reaches 350 degrees, remove pan from heat. Cut the butter into chunks. Carefully stir in the butter one piece at a time—the mixture will bubble up somewhat violently at this point. Continue stirring until all of the butter is melted and fully incorporated into the sugar mix.

Once butter is incorporated, slowly and carefully pour the cream into the pot—the mixture will once again bubble up. Stir well, until cream is completely incorporated, leaving you with a thick, smooth sauce. Mix in the sea salt, and allow mixture to cool for 20 minutes or so.

Pour sauce into glass jar(s) and allow to cool to room temperature before covering with a lid. Store in the fridge; warm and stir briefly when ready to use. ◊

BLUEBERRY SAUCE

This sauce is particularly tasty served over Sweet Corn Ice Cream (page 112) or layered with Sweet Corn Mousse (page 108) for a unique and beautiful parfait. **MAKES ABOUT 2 CUPS**

....

 1 pint fresh blueberries (about 2 cups)
 ¾ cup granulated sugar
 ⅔ cup water
 2 teaspoons fresh lemon juice
 ½–1 teaspoon vanilla extract

....

Combine blueberries, sugar, water, and lemon juice in a medium saucepan. Bring to a boil, stirring frequently. Reduce heat and simmer until the blueberries have broken down into a thick sauce, about 20 minutes. Remove from heat; stir in vanilla extract, and cool to room temperature. Transfer cooled blueberry sauce to a jar; chill until serving.

Variations

• Add the zest of 1 orange along with the lemon juice.

• Try substituting amaretto liqueur for all or part of the water— delicious! ◇

Index